George Washington

Chosen

By

God?

Robert W. Pelton
$14.95

Jacket design: Kathleen Pelton
kafleenvs@aol.com

Printed in the United States of America
On Recycled Paper

Freedom & Liberty Foundation Press
First Edition

Dedication

    Some earlier members of my family to whom I dedicate this book are as follows: Front row left to right my Great-Great Grandfather Elias Mitchell and his wife, Sarah; my Grandmother Olive. Back row left to right my Great Uncle Arthur, Great Aunt Mary, Great Uncle Albert and Great Aunt Goldie.

CONTENTS

1

Meet

The Father

Of

Our Country

President of the Constitutional Convention

Some Important Highlights

Few people realize that George Washington (1732 – 1799) was a man who formally attended school only to the elementary level. Yet, he went on to become Commander-in-Chief of the Continental Army in 1775, and served in this capacity until 1783.

Washington first gained prominence leading troops from Virginia in support of the British Empire during the French and Indian War (1754–1763), a conflict which he inadvertently helped to start.

After leading the American victory in the Revolutionary War, he relinquished his military power and returned to civilian life. This act alone brought him much renown.

There was initially a question as to how the new leader was to be properly addressed. The Senate proposed that he be called *"King"* or as *"His Highness the President of the United States and Protector of Their Liberties."* Washington refused to consider either of these titles. As a result, the Senate and the House of Representatives, after much heated debate, compromised and agreed on the use of the much less pompous *"President of the United States."*

After his second term expired, Washington again retired to civilian life. He thereby established an important precedent of peaceful change of government that was to serve as an example for the United States and for future Republics throughout the world.

Because of his central role in the founding of the United States, Washington is often called the *"Father of the Country."* Scholars rank him among the greatest of United States presidents.

Washington's Faith in God

Washington's Spiritual Life

Here is what he in turn said about her: *"My mother was the most beautiful woman I ever saw. All I am I owe to my mother. I attribute all my success in life to the moral, intellectual and physical education I received from her."*

He'd stand up at promptly 9:00 pm, take his candle, and go off by himself. There, from 9:00pm to 10:00pm, he wouldn't be seen. He was alone on his knees in front of a chair praying. A candle stood on a stand next to the chair. And his **Bible** was open before him. This he would do even when guests were present. Then promptly at 10:00pm, he would emerge and go directly to his bedroom.

He'd get up every morning at 4:00am, and spend another hour in the same room. He could be found kneeling before the same chair, in the same posture, with the same *Bible* open before him.

William White comments on the personal life of Washington's in his book, *Washington's Writing:* *"It seems proper to subjoin to this letter what was told to me by Mr. Robert Lewis, at Fredericksburg, in the year 1827. Being a nephew of Washington, and his private secretary during the first part of his presidency, Mr. Lewis lived with him on terms of intimacy, and had the best opportunity for observing his habits.*

"Mr. Lewis said that he had accidentally witnessed his private devotions in his library both morning and evening; that on those occasions he had seen him in a kneeling posture with a Bible open before him, and that he believed such to have been his daily practice."

Washington made a practice of never traveling unnecessarily on the Sabbath. He never, no matter what the circumstances, received visitors on Sunday, with one exception, a Godly friend named Trumbel. They would spend time reading the *Bible* and praying together.

Henry Muhlenberg was the pastor of the Lutheran church near Valley Forge. He also was one of the founders of the Lutheran Church in America. He said this about Washington while he was in command of the Continental Army: *"I heard a fine example today, namely, that His Excellency General Washington rode around among his army yesterday and admonished each and every one to fear God, to put away the wickedness that has set in and become so general, and to practice the Christian virtues. From all appearances, this gentleman does not belong to the so-called world of society, for he respects God's Word, believes in the atonement through Christ, and bears himself in humility and gentleness. Therefore, the Lord God has also singularly, yea, marvelously, preserved him from harm in the midst of countless perils, ambuscades, fatigues, etc., and has hitherto graciously held him in His hand as a chosen vessel."*

Praying at Valley Forge

The paintings of George Washington kneeling in prayer in the snow covered woods of

Valley Forge are based on fact. We have all probably heard of his prayer that was overheard by a Quaker, a pacifist, a Tory – a man loyal to the Crown. This man returned home shaken and said to his wife: *"Our cause is lost! I came unexpectedly in the woods upon a man who was kneeling in prayer. As I drew closer, I heard his voice. I heard the impassioned plea of his prayers and saw the tears on his cheeks. I knew our cause was lost."*

The Quaker and his wife were so overwhelmed that they became supporters of Washington and the American cause.

A slightly different version of this same story comes from William J. Fedder's **America's God and Country**:

"In 1777 while the American army lay at Valley Forge, a good old Quaker by the name of Potts had occasion to pass through a thick woods near headquarters. As he traversed the dark brown forest, he heard, at a distance before him, a voice which as he advanced became more fervid ... .

"Approaching with slowness and circumspection, whom should he behold in a dark bower, apparently formed for the purpose, but the Commander-in-Chief of the armies of the United Colonies on his knees in the act of devotion to the Ruler of the Universe!

"At the moment when Friend Potts, concealed by the trees, came up, Washington was

14

interceding for his beloved country. With tones of gratitude that labored for adequate expression he adored that exuberant goodness which, from the depth of obscurity, had exalted him to the head of a great nation, and that nation fighting at fearful odds for all the world holds dear.

"Soon as the General had finished his devotions and had retired, Friend Potts returned to his house, and threw himself into a chair by the side of his wife. 'Heigh! Isaac!' said she with tenderness, 'thee seems agitated; what's the matter?'

"'Indeed, my dear' quoth he, 'if I appear agitated 'tis no more than what I have seen this day what I shall never forget. Till now I have bought that a Christian and a soldier were characters incompatible; but if George Washington be not a man of God, l am mistaken, and still more shall I be disappointed if God does not through him perform some great thing for this country.'"

Washington's Oath and Actions

To Be Condemned
As Traitors to the Crown

General Washington, the 56 Signers of the *Declaration of Independence* and the 39 Signers of the **Constitution** (of which he was one), or for that matter any Colonist who bore arms or agitated for Independence, were condemned as traitors by the vengeful British.

Should the struggle for Independence fail, an ignominious *(humiliating, disgraceful, contemptible, shameful)* death by hanging would most certainly be their punishment.

Despite the fact that every man knew his possible fate, not one became a turncoat! Not one took Gage's offer! In fact, each man was unwavering and most courageous.

Yet this great American patriot didn't have the honor of signing the *Declaration of Independence.* He certainly would have done so had the opportunity presented itself. Then why did he not sign the grand document?

George Washington was not in attendance at the *Continental Congress* when the *Declaration* was signed. He was at the time Commander-in Chief of the Continental Army and far away serving in this capacity.

Regarding George Washington, John Grady, a physician and former United States Navy jet pilot has this to say: *"Because of the devotion and vision of one man, and the loyalty and courage of a small force of fighting Americans -- the course of history was forever changed."*

And so it was!

A British Leader's Comment

Yes, this is the man who was so highly honored by the great British statesman and four times Prime Minister, William Gladstone.

Gladstone once proposed the creation of a grouping of pedestals for statues of history's greatest men.

The pedestal in the center was noticeably higher that the others.

Gladstone was asked to identify the figure to be given the place of honor on the highest pedestal.

Without a moment's hesitation, he answered: *"George Washington."*

2

Little Known Things About the Father of Our Country

**An exact likeness of Washington.
Made from an impression of his face
while he was still alive.**

George Washington
(1732 – 1799)

Heritage

English. Born in Wakefield Plantation, Virginia.

Eldest of six children from his father's first marriage.

Only 11 when father died.

Ancestry can be traced back to several lines of British royalty.

Religion

Christian. Born and raised in a Godly home.

Mother taught him the *Bible* and how to pray.

Father taught him to know and worship God.

Marriage

Married Martha Dandridge Custis, an extremely wealthy widow.

She had two children from her previous marriage.

He was 26 and she was 27 at the time.

Children

He and Martha had no children.

He brought up Martha's children as if they were his own.

Interesting Highlights

Inherited Mount Vernon when 20 years old..

Had at least 166 head of prize cattle at Mount Vernon in 1765.

Switched from growing tobacco to grain in the 1760s.

One of largest land holders in Virginia.

One of wealthiest men in the Colonies.

Made numerous and generous loans of money to friends in need.

Selected to be *Commander-in-Chief of the Continental Army* in 1775 after the battles of Lexington and Concord.

This took place at the Pennsylvania State House in Philadelphia where:

Declaration of Independence was later signed in 1776.

Articles of Confederation were adopted as our first *Constitution in* 1781. *Constitutional Convention* was held in 1787.

Four-star general while in command of the *Continental Army.*

Promoted posthumously to rank of six-star *General of the Armies of Congress.*

Done under an order given by President Jimmy Carter.

Instituted a special combat medal he called the *"Badge of Courage"* during the War for American Independence.

This was the forerunner of today's *"Purple Heart"* and the *"Congressional Medal of Honor."*

Forbid his troops from using profanity.

Required his troops to regularly attend church services.

He and James Madison were the only signers to later become President.

Was a half first cousin twice removed from Madison.

One of 12 Signers of the Constitution who owned slaves. Others were:

Richard Bassett (Delaware)
John Blair (Virginia)
William Blount (North Carolina)
Pierce Butler (South Carolina)
Daniel Carroll (Maryland)
Daniel of St. Thomas Jenifer (Maryland)
James Madison (Virginia)
Charles Pinckney (South Carolina)
Charles Cotesworth Pinckney (South Carolina)
John Rutledge (South Carolina)
Richard Dobbs Spaight, Sr. (North Carolina)

Delegate from Virginia to the *First* and *Second Continental Congress.*

Chosen to be first President of the United States.

Received all nine votes of the electoral college which was made up of representatives from each State.

Only President in our history to have been unanimously elected.

There was no such thing at this time as a *"popular vote"* for President.

Our nation's capitol was moved from New York to Philadelphia during his Presidency.

Only President of the United States to be inaugurated in two different cities.

New York City in April of 1789.

Philadelphia in March of 1793.

Only President who didn't live in the White House.

Elected without belonging to a political party.

When elected President there was still:
a *King* in France
a *Czar* in Russia
an *Emperor* in China
a *Shogun* in Japan

Borrowed money to get to his inauguration.

Wore When Inaugurated

This is what he wore when sworn in on April 30, 1789, while on the balcony of Federal Hall in New York City:

Dark brown suit
Steel-hilted sword
White silk stockings
Silver shoe buckles

His *Second Inaugural Address* was given in the Senate Chamber of Congress Hall in Philadelphia on March 4, 1793, was shortest in American history.

When inaugurated, Washington was wearing:
Black velvet suit.
Diamond knee buckles.
Black silk stockings.
Silver shoe buckles.
Dress sword with richly ornamented hilt.

His Teeth

Had only one real tooth when inaugurated. All the others were false.

They were carved at different times from the following:

deer antlers

whale bone
rhinoceros ivory

Other Interesting Tidbits

His *Farewell Address* in 1796 was never delivered orally.

It was printed in the newspaper.

Used to take boat from Mount Vernon to Washington, D.C. to get to work.

Known to be a workaholic.

Took time off now and then to go fishing.

Favorite fish was the shad.

Loved to go fox hunting when time permitted.

Liked to explore caves.

Had six white horses in his stable.

Before riding he insisted that his horse be cleaned from head to hoof.

His horse's teeth had to be brushed daily.

His dog was named *"Sweet Lips."*

Denounced the idea that the *Continental Army* should take over the newly formed government.

There was a proposal at the *Constitutional Convention* to limit the standing army in the country to 5,000 men.

Washington sarcastically agreed so long as a stipulation was added that no invading army could number more than 3,000 troops!

References to God

Used more than 80 different names in reference to God in his prayers and his writings. They included:

Almighty Being
All Wise Dispenser of Events

Beneficent Author of the Universe
the God of Armies

Author of All Good
Eternal Lord God

Most Gracious God
Thy Divine Majesty

King of Heaven

"So Help Me God," following the required oath of office was initiated by Washington.

His picture was the first of our Presidents to appear on a postage stamp.

Did his own bookkeeping.

Carefully recorded every penny of expenditures and profits

Supervised the planning to relocate the government in the District of Columbia.

Played an important role in the development of the new federal city that was to be named after him.

Oversaw the design of the new Capitol Building and the White House.

Laid the cornerstone of the Capitol in 1793.

Foreign Travels

Visited only one foreign country during his lifetime.

This was Barbados in the West Indies when he was 19 years old.

Made the trip with older half-brother, Lawrence.

Washington hoped the warmer climate would help his brother's failing health.

Unfortunately, Lawrence died within a year.

Pushed for the passage of the first U.S. Patent Act in 1789 as President (1789-97).

Signed the first official US patent to Samuel Hopkins of Philadelphia.

This was for his process of making potash and pearl ash.

Established a *Corps of Artillerists and Engineers* in 1794 to be stationed at West Point, New York.

This later become the United States Military Academy at West Point.

Suffered from following ailments during his lifetime:

Malaria

Small pox

Tuberculosis

Dysentery

Pneumonia

His face was scarred from small pox.

Died of a throat infection at Mount Vernon on December 14, 1779.

It was some time after 10:00pm.

He was 67 years old.

Only President to die in the 1700s.

Left no direct descendant as he never sired a child to continue his line.

Quotable Quote

"Firearms stand next in importance to the Constitution itself. They are the American people's liberty teeth. ... The very atmosphere of firearms everywhere restrains evil interference."

"When firearms go, all goes – we need them every hour."

Little Known Facts:

First Mason to serve as President.

Introduced the mule to America.

Never shook hands during his entire two Presidential terms.

Believed this was beneath the dignity of a President.

Had two ice cream freezers constructed and installed in his Mount Vernon home.

Owned 123 slaves upon his death.

According to his *Will*, all of his slaves were to be given their freedom upon the death of Martha.

One special slave, William, called *"my mulatto man,"* was given the choice of freedom or to stay at Mount Vernon.

William was to be taken care of for the rest of his life.

William received an annuity of $30.00

He also was given all the clothing and food he was accustomed to getting.

Physical Attributes

6-2" tall and about 175 pounds.

Weight went up to about 200 pounds later in life.

Wore size 13 boots.

Refused to wear a powdered wig although they were fashionable at the time.

Wore his reddish-brown hair in a short braid down his back.

Powdered his hair.

Price Paid for Signing

All the Signers, including Washington, suffered monetary losses because of their connection with the cause.

Much of Washington's extensive fortune was lost due to financial sacrifices and long absences during the war.

Favorite Cologne

Have you ever heard of *Caswell Massey No. 6*? Probably not! It's a little piece of history that few people would know. But it's interesting nevertheless. Why? Because it's the cologne used by George Washington while he was the Commander-in-Chief of the *Continental Army*; as well as while he was the President of the United States.

General Washington allowed his close friend, French General Lafayette, to use some while he was here in the Colonies fighting for the American cause. So much did Lafayette like this cologne that Washington later shipped a case to him in Paris to thank him for French support during the American Revolution.

It's still produced by *Caswell-Massey, Co. Ltd. Chemists and Perfumers.* The company calls itself:*" The oldest chemists and perfumers in America. Established in 1752."* This is 24 years before John Hancock boldly and courageously affixed his name to our glorious *Declaration of Independence*! In fact, John was no more than a 15 year old teenager at that time.

What's So Special About Friday?

You no doubt know many interesting things about George Washington, but what do you know about Friday and the Father of our Country? We all know that Friday has been considered *"unlucky"* for centuries because the crucifixion occurred on Friday. But, regarding George Washington, consider these Friday facts:

He was born on Friday.

Commissioned a lieutenant colonel.

Took command of the Army of Virginia.

Elected Commander-in-Chief.

Fought the Battle of Princeton..

Won the victory at Yorktown.

Elected President of the Constitutional Convention.

Created the War Department.

Created the State Department.

Appointed his first cabinet officer.

Proclaimed the first national Thanksgiving and at that time said: *"It is the duty of all nations to acknowledge the Providence of Almighty God, to obey His will, to be grateful for His benefits and humbly to implore His protection and favor."*

The First Submarine

During the Revolutionary War, Washington sent David Bushnell's hand operated submarine into New York Harbor to sink a British warship. The Turtle's lone operator attempted to attach a timed bomb to the British Eagle's hull. The mission failed when the bomb floated away before exploding. The technology just wasn't advanced enough for

Washington's vision. Therefore, submarines didn't become a force in navies for the next 100 years.

On June 9, 1778, at Valley Forge, Pennsylvania, George Washington issued a call for engineers and engineering education. This order is considered the genesis of a *US Army Engineer School*, which found its permanent home at Fort Belvoir, Virginia, where Washington had practiced surveying.

Washington was a successful commercial fisherman and an innovator whose harvesting and selective-breeding concepts changed the face of 18th-century farming. He was a cutting-edge businessman who was experimenting with things long before anyone else tried.

Washington's Grist Mill

George Washington first acquired a gristmill when he inherited Mount Vernon from the widow of his half-brother, Lawrence, in 1754. This first business enterprise was a *"custom mill"* where wheat and corn were ground for sale to neighboring farmers and, for consumption on his Estate.

Washington was an entrepreneur and in 1770, he decided to build a *"merchant mill,"* which began operation the following year. Here flour and cornmeal were ground, not only for use at Mount Vernon, but also to sell up and down the East Coast of America and as far away as Portugal and the West Indies. The new mill had two pairs of stones. One was used to grind wheat into flour, and the other pair was used to grind corn into meal.

Water to operate for the grist mill came from Dogue Run stream. Flour was loaded onto ships from a wharf located on the stream's waterfront. At this same location, Washington ran a distillery for making whiskey, and a cooperage, where barrels were made for storing and shipping the products produced at the site.

Making Whiskey at Mount Vernon

After Washington left the Presidency, he returned to Mount Vernon. He did more than just pace the grounds of his huge estate wondering what he should do next. His farm manager, John Anderson, was a master distiller from Scotland. Anderson suggested building a whiskey distillery to make use of grain in danger of being eaten by mice or rotting.

Washington followed Anderson's advice and built his distillery. This distillery and a larger one he built a year later, soon made the Father of Our Country the biggest whiskey distributor in the newly formed United States. It was produced in large quantities all year around.

In 1999, archaeologists excavated the foundation of the 206-year-old distillery. Its blueprints were soon after discovered in Washington's meticulous records. It was a 75-by-30-foot building and had been solidly constructed of local sandstone. At its peak, it was packed with:

> five copper stills
>
> five worm tubes *(copper tubes that collected condensed distillate)*
>
> a boiler
>
> 50 mash tubs

Here are a few unique facts about this man who was fast becoming one of the countries first successful entrepreneurs:

He created his own special recipe for making rye whiskey.

11,000 gallons of liquor were produced in 1798, the year before he died.

His profit was $7,500, a huge sum in those days.

His distillery's made the equivalent of $300,000 over a two year period.

One of his ledgers show that cinnamon, persimmon and other flavoring agents were sometimes added.

Under aged corn whiskey *(today known as "moonshine")* made up of around 90 percent of his whiskey production and sales.

He also experimented with varying qualities of whiskey. Small quantities of at least six kinds were produced. These higher whiskey grades made up the remaining 10 percent of his total.

A limited amount of specialty grades of whiskey were made only during the summer and fall. These were classed as:

Common	Fine Rectified
Strong Proof	Rectified
Rye Whiskey	Rectified 4th Proof

Some of this special grade whiskey was set aside for use on the plantation for use when entertaining guests. Most was shipped off to as many as 270 customers. They included:

merchants　　grocers　　innkeepers

Those who purchased Washington's whiskey for personal consumption or for their slaves and employees included:

neighbors	boatmen	planters
overseers	a weaver	a butcher
	a cartwright	

Many of Washington's customers paid for their liquor in cash. Others bartered with a great variety of things including:

corn   rye   wheat,

salt   clover seed

Still others accepted a quantity of whiskey as payment or partial payment for their services. These included:

His personal physician   a seamstress

People contracted to do specific jobs.

Most of his whiskey clientele were from such places as:

Alexandria   Richmond

Maryland counties neighboring Mount Vernon.

Virginia counties neighboring Mount Vernon.

It's not known if Washington drank his own whiskey.

He was a light drinker who favored rum and fortified wines.

Washington was convinced of the beneficial effects of alcohol on his troops as they were battling the British.

As he wrote to a congressional leader in 1777: *"The benefits from moderate use of liquor have been experienced in all armies and are not to be disputed."*

Or, as he instructed the commissary general of purchases for the Continental Army in 1777: *"There should always be a sufficient quantity of spirits with the army, to furnish moderate supplies to the troops ... such as when they are marching in hot or cold weather, in camp in wet, on fatigue or in working parties, it is so essential that it is not to be dispensed with."*

Washington's thriving liquor business was profitable. This particular enterprise helped finance operations of his sprawling Mount Vernon plantation. When he died in December of 1799, the distillery became the property of his nephew. Lawrence allowed the business to decline until it was no longer of any worth.

Washington's Last Will and Testament

"In the name of God, Amen. All my debts, of which there are but few, and none of magnitude are to be punctually and speedily paid. To my dearly beloved wife, Martha Washington, I give and bequeath the use, profit, and benefit of my whole estate, real and personal, for the term of her natural life. Upon the decease of my wife it is my will and desire that all slaves whom I hold in my own right shall receive their freedom. And to my mulatto man, William (calling himself William Lee), I give

immediate freedom, or, if he should prefer it (on account of the accidents which have befallen him, and which have rendered him incapable of walking, or of any active employment), to remain in the situation he now is, it shall be optional in him to do so: In either case, however, I allow him an annuity of thirty dollars during his natural life, which shall be independent of the victuals and clothes he has been accustomed to receive, if he choose the last alternative; but in full with his freedom if he prefers the first: and this I give him, as a testimony of my sense of his attachment to me, and for his faithful services during the Revolutionary War."

The Inscription on His Tomb

Taken from the *Book of John, Chapter 11, Verses 25-26*:

"I am the Resurrection and the Life; saith the Lord. He that believeth in Me, though he were dead yet shall he live. And whosoever liveth and believeth in Me shall never die."

The Washington Monument

The beautiful and towering Washington Monument in Washington, D.C., stands over 555 feet high. These words, befitting the Founder of our country, are engraved on the metal cap: *"Praise be to God"*.

3

Jefferson a Christian?

His Letter Describes

His Friend

Was Thomas Jefferson a Christian? Or was he a deist as many of today's most influential historians claim? Why not let Mr. Jefferson speak for himself in this regard. These are his exact words: *"I am a real Christian, … a disciple of the doctrines of Jesus. … I am a Christian in the*

only sense in which He wished anyone to be, sincerely attached to His doctrine in preference to all others."

Could it be any clearer than this?

What man could possibly be better qualified to tell of George Washington's character than Thomas Jefferson? After all, he and Washington had been closely associated before, during and after those critical years of the American Revolution. Both of these great Americans mutually toiled and sacrificed for many years during the monumental struggle to bring about the founding of the greatest nation to ever grace the face of the earth, bar none.

And lastly, both men played such important roles pertaining to two of our nations most important documents. Jefferson created the initial draft of the momentous *Declaration of Independence* and he signed the document as well. Washington couldn't sign as he was at the time, Commander-in-Chief of the Continental Army. He was away and busily fighting a war against a most unwelcome and off times, vengeful British invader, an invader hell bent on punishing the upstart Colonists.

Washington, on the other hand, would later become the President of the *Constitutional Convention*, and played a most important part in almost miraculously guiding the grand document through to its adoption.

The material to follow was excerpted from a descriptive letter written to Dr. Walter Jones on January 2, 1814. Jefferson pulls no punches in giving his frank description of the *"Father of Our Country."*

Jefferson's Letter Regarding His Friend

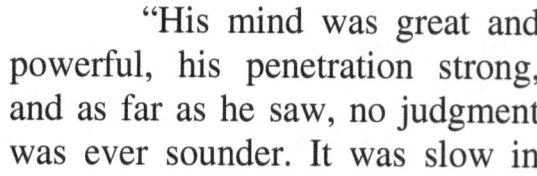

"I knew General Washington intimately and thoroughly; and were I called on to delineate his character, it would be in terms like these:

"His mind was great and powerful, his penetration strong, and as far as he saw, no judgment was ever sounder. It was slow in operation, being little aided by invention or imagination, but sure in conclusion. Hence the common remark of his officers, of the advantage he derived from councils of war, where hearing all suggestions he selected whatever was best; and certainly no general ever planned his battles more judiciously.

"He was incapable of fear, meeting personal dangers with the calmest unconcern. Perhaps the strongest feature in his character was prudence, never acting until every circumstance, every consideration, was maturely weighed; refraining if he saw a doubt, but when once decided, going through with his purpose, whatever obstacles opposed.

"His integrity was most pure, his justice the most inflexible I have ever known, no motives of interest or consanguinity, of friendship or hatred, being able to bias his decision. He was, indeed, in every sense of the words, a wise, a good, and a great man.

"His temper was naturally high toned; but reflection and resolution has obtained a firm and habitual ascendancy over it. If ever, however, it broke its bonds, he was most tremendous in wrath.

"In his expenses he was honorable, but exact; liberal in contributions to whatever promised utility; but frowning and unyielding on all visionary projects and all unworthy projects and all unworthy calls on his charity. His heart was not warm in its affections; but he exactly calculated every man's value, and gave him a solid esteem proportioned to it.

"His person, as you know, was fine, his stature exactly what one would wish, his deportment easy, erect and noble; the best horseman of his age, and the most graceful figure that could be seen on horseback.

"He wrote readily, rather diffusely, in an easy and correct style. This he had acquired by conversation with the world, for his education was merely reading, writing, and common arithmetic, to which he added surveying at a later day. His time was employed in action chiefly.

"On the whole, his character was, in its mass, perfect, in nothing bad, in few points indifferent; and it may truly be said, that never did nature and fortune combine more perfectly to make a man great, and to place him in the same constellation with whatever worthies have merited from man by an everlasting remembrance.

"For his was the singular destiny and merit of leading the armies of his country successfully through an arduous war, for the establishment of its independence; of conducting its councils through the birth of a government, new in its forms and principles, until it had settled down into a quiet and orderly train; and of scrupulously obeying the laws through the whole of his career, civil and military, of which the history of the world furnishes no other example."

And Two Centuries Later

David McCullough, a writer, a historian, more than two centuries later, logically analyzed and then carefully interpreted many of the facts he accumulated during his extensive research for his marvelous book, **1776**. Yet his conclusions, however honest they might be, are sometimes found to greatly be at odds with the above views of Thomas Jefferson. And Jefferson actually spent much time with Washington and knew him intimately. Here are some of the things McCullough wrongly declared:

1.) *"Washington was prone to **self-doubt** and flashes of **self-pity**."*
*"Washington was **insecure** …"*
I remind you of Jefferson' words: *"**He was incapable of fear, meeting personal danger with the calmest unconcern.**"*
"Self-doubt?" **"Self pity?"** **"Insecure?"** How could Washington, a man **"incapable of fear,"** possess any of these problems?

2.) *"He was not a **rilliant** **strategist** or tactician ... not an **intellectual**. ... he had **made** serious mistakes in judgment."*

Jefferson again: *"**Certainly no General ever planned his battles more judiciously. ... His mind was great and powerful, his penetration strong. ... no judgment was sounder.**"*

I ask you this about General Washington: Not a **brilliant strategist?** Not an **intellectual?** Made **serious mistakes in judgment?**

3.) *"At several crucial moments he showed marked indecisiveness."*

Jefferson: *"**Perhaps the strongest feature in his character was prudence, never acting until every circumstance, every consideration, was maturely verified ... but when once decided, going through with his purpose, whatever obstacles opposed.**"*

Does this sound like a man burdened by **"marked indecisiveness?"**

I think you will agree that above examples clearly show how a writer, a historian, more than two centuries later, could logically interpret the facts he gathers together in his extensive research. Yet his interpretation, however honest his intent might be, differs greatly with the views of a man who was actually there at the time.

4

A Christian Leader's

Quotable Quotes

On July 8, 1755, just after a bloody enemy encounter, Washington wrote to his brother, John A. Washington: *"But by the all-powerful dispensations of Providence, I have been protected beyond all human probability or expectation; for I had four bullets through my coat, and two horses shot under me, yet escaped unhurt, although death was leveling my companions on every side of me!"*

It was a time when the Colonial leaders were trying to decide whether or not to cut their ties with England. Washington wrote this in his diary on June 1, 1774: *"Went to church and fasted all day."*

Washington gave this order on July 4, 1775, while in his headquarters at Cambridge: *"The General most earnestly requires and expects a due observance of those articles of war established for the government of the Army which forbid profane cursing, swearing and drunkenness. And in like manner he requires and expects of all officers and soldiers not engaged in actual duty, a punctual attendance of Divine services, to implore the blessing of Heaven upon the means used for our safety and defense."*

On July 9, 1776, the Continental Congress authorized the providing of chaplains for Continental Army. General Washington immediately gave the order to appoint a chaplain to every regiment of the Continental Army: *"The General hopes and trusts that every officer and man, will endeavor so to live, and act, as becomes a Christian Soldier defending the dearest Rights and Liberties of his country."*

This order was issued by Washington on July 20,1776: *"The General orders this day to be religiously observed by the forces under his Command, exactly in manner directed by the Continental Congress. It is therefore strictly enjoined on all officers and soldiers to attend Divine service. And it is expected that all those who go to worship do take their arms, ammunition and accoutrements, and are prepared for immediate action, if called upon."*

On May 2, 1778, General George Washington was with his troops at Valley Forge He declared: *"While we are zealously performing the duties of good citizens and soldiers, we certainly ought not to be inattentive to the higher duties of religion.*

"To the distinguished character of Patriot, it should be our highest Glory to laud the more distinguished Character of Christian.

"The signal instances of Providential goodness which we have experienced and which have now almost crowned our labors with complete success

demand from us in a peculiar manner the warmest returns of gratitude and piety to the Supreme Author of all good."

On August 20, 1778, General George Washington wrote a letter to Brigadier-General Thomas Nelson in Virginia. He told his long time friend: *"The hand of Providence has been so conspicuous in all this (the course of the war) that he must be worse than an infidel that lacks faith, and more wicked that has not gratitude to acknowledge his obligations; but it will be time enough for me to turn Preacher when my present appointment ceases.*"

British troops under Lord Cornwallis surrendered at Yorktown on October 19, 1781. On October 20, Washington ordered a special church service to give thanks to God: *"The commander-in-chief earnestly recommends that the troops not on duty should universally attend with that seriousness of deportment and gratitude of heart which the recognition of such reiterated and astonishing interposition of Providence demands of us.*"

General Washington wrote to Thomas McKean, President of the Continental Congress, on November 15, 1781: *"I take a particular pleasure in acknowledging that the interposing Hand of Heaven, in the various instances of our extensive Preparation for this Operation (Yorktown), has been most conspicuous and remarkable.*"

When the Revolutionary War finally ended, General Washington wrote a farewell letter to the 13 Governors of the newly freed states. It was sent from his headquarters in Newburgh, New York, and dated June 14, 1783. In it he stated: *"I now make it my earnest prayer that God would have you, and the State over which you preside, in his holy protection...that he would most graciously be pleased to dispose us all to do justice, to love, mercy, and to demean ourselves with that charity, humility, and pacific temper of mind, which were the characteristics of the Divine Author of our blessed religion, and without an humble imitation of whose example in these things, we can never hope to be a happy nation.*"

General Washington addressed Congress while at the Capitol of Maryland in Annapolis on December 23, 1783. His speech was with regard to the official resignation of his military commission: *"I resign with satisfaction the appointment ... my abilities to accomplish so arduous a task, were superseded by ... the patronage of Heaven. My gratitude for the interposition of Providence ... increases with every review of the momentous contest. ...*

"*I consider it an indispensable duty to close this last solemn act of my Official life by commending the Interest of our dearest Country to the protection of Almighty God, and those who have the superintendence of them, to His holy keeping.*"

"*The pew I hold in the Episcopal Church at Alexandria, shall be charged with an annual rent of five pounds, Virginia money; and I promise to pay annually, to the minister and vestry of the Protestant Episcopal Church in Fairfax parish.*" (April 25th, 1785)

General Benjamin Lincoln was a deputy to George Washington during the Revolutionary War. He was the officer who was instructed to accept the sword from General Cornwallis when the British surrendered at Yorktown. Lincoln received a letter from General Washington dated June 29, 1788, that read: "*No Country upon Earth ever had it more in its power to attain these blessings. ... Much to be regretted indeed would it be, were we to neglect the means and depart from the road which Providence has pointed us to, so plainly; I cannot believe it will ever come to pass. The Great Governor of the Universe has led us too long and too far. .. . to forsake us in the midst of it. ... We may, now and then, get bewildered; but I hope and trust that there is good sense and virtue enough left to recover the right path."*

Jonathan Trumbul was the British Governor of Connecticut who changed sides and became a strong supporter of America's quest for independence. Washington wrote this man on July 20, 1788, and said in part: *"We may, with a kind of grateful and pious exultation, trace the finger of Providence through those dark and mysterious events, which first induced the States to appoint a general Convention and then led them one after another into an adoption of the system recommended by that general Convention; thereby in all human probability, laying a lasting foundation for tranquility and happiness."*

April 30, 1789, George Washington was prepared to take the oath of office. He stood with his hand on an open **Bible** while the on the balcony of Federal Hall, in New York City. Embarrassed by the loudly pealing church bells, the booming cannon noise and the deafening ovation, he went inside to deliver his Inaugural Speech to both Houses of Congress. The new President proclaimed in part: *"Such being the impressions under which I have, in obedience to the public summons, repaired to the present station, it would be peculiarly improper to omit, in this first official act, my fervent* *supplications to that Almighty Being who rules over the universe, who presides in the councils of nations and whose providential aids can supply every human defect, that His benediction may consecrate to the liberties and happiness of the people of the United States a Government instituted by themselves for these essential purposes; and may enable every instrument employed in its administration to execute with success, the functions allotted to his charge.*

"In tendering this homage to the Great Author of every public and private good, I assure myself that it expresses your sentiments not less than my own; nor those of my fellow-citizens at large, less than either.

"No people can be bound to acknowledge and adore the Invisible Hand which conducts the affairs of men more than the people of the United States.

"Every step by which they have advanced to the character of an independent nation seems to have been distinguished by some token of providential agency."

Washington once declared to an assembly of the Episcopal Church: *"That Government alone can be approved by Heaven, which promotes peace and secures protection to its Citizens in every thing that is dear and interesting to them. ... "*

The Quakers were holding their annual get-

together at for Maryland, Delaware, New Jersey, Pennsylvania and the western part of Virginia in October of 1789. President Washington addressed them in this manner: *"The liberty enjoyed by the People of these States of worshipping Almighty God agreeable to their consciences is not only among the choicest of their blessings, but also of their rights.*
"While men perform their social duties faithfully, they do all that society or the state can with propriety demand or expect; and remain responsible only to their Maker for the religion, or modes of faith, which they may prefer or profess."

A *National Day of Thanksgiving Proclamation* was issued by Washington on October 3, 1789, in which he said in part: *"Whereas it is the duty of all nations to acknowledge the providence of Almighty God, to obey His will, to be grateful for his benefits, and humbly to implore His protection and favor. ... Now therefore, I do recommend and assign Thursday, the twenty-sixth day of November next, to be devoted by the people of these United States. ... that we then may all unite unto him our sincere and humble thanks for His kind care and protection of the people of this country previous to their becoming a nation; for the signal and manifold mercies and the favorable interpositions of His providence in the course and conclusion of the late war; ..."*

In a letter of March 11, 1792, President Washington wrote: *"I am sure that never was a people, who had more reason to acknowledge a Divine interposition in their affairs, than those of the United States; and I should be pained to believe that they have forgotten that agency, which was so often manifested during our Revolution, or that they failed to consider the omnipotence of that God who is alone able to protect them."*

In a letter to the congregation of the **New Christian Church** in Baltimore, Maryland, President George Washington exclaimed on January 27, 1793: *"We have abundant reason to rejoice that in this Land the light of truth and reason has triumphed over the power of bigotry and superstition, and that every person may here worship God according to the dictates of his own heart. In this enlightened Age and in this Land of equal liberty it is our boast, that a man's religious tenets will not forfeit the protection of the Laws, nor deprive him of the right of attaining and holding the highest offices that are known in the United States."*

Another **National Day of Thanksgiving Proclamation** was issued by President Washington on January 1, 1795: *"It is in an especial manner our duty as a people, with devout reverence and affectionate gratitude, to acknowledge our many and* *great obligations to Almighty God, and to implore Him to continue and confirm the blessings we experienced. ... "Deeply penetrated with this sentiment, I, George Washington, President of the United States, do recommend to all religious societies and denominations, and to all persons whomsoever within the United States, to set apart and observe Thursday, the 19th day of February next, as a day of public thanksgiving and prayer."*

Other Quotes of Great interest

"May the same wonder-working Deity, who long since delivering the Hebrews from their Egyptian Oppressors planted them in the promised land—whose providential agency has lately been conspicuous in establishing these United States as an independent Nation—still continue to water them with the dews of Heaven and to make the inhabitants of every denomination participate in the temporal and spiritual blessings of that people whose God is Jehovah."

"As the contempt of the religion of a country, by ridiculing any of its ceremonies, or affronting its Ministers ... , has ever been deeply resented, you are to be particularly careful, to restrain every officer and soldier from such

imprudence and folly, and to punish every instance of it."

"The blessing and protection of Heaven are, at a times, necessary; but, especially so, in times of public distress and danger."

"Liberty, honor, and safety, are all at stake; and, trust, Providence will smile upon our efforts, and establish us, once more, the inhabitants of a free and happy country."

"In having pleased the Almighty Ruler of the Universe, to defend the cause of the United American States, and finally to raise us up a powerful friend among the Princes of the earth, to establish our liberty and independency upon a lasting foundation."

"It will ever be the first wish of my heart, to inculcate a due sense of the dependence we ought to place in that All-Wise and. Powerful Being, on whom alone our success depends."

"In no instance, since the commencement of the war, has the interposition of Providence appeared more remarkably conspicuous, than in the rescue of the post and garrison of West Point from Arnold's villainous perfidy. I most devoutly

congratulate my country, and every well-wisher to the cause, on this signal stroke of Providence."

"The Commander-in-chief earnestly recommends, that the troops not on duty should universally attend, with that seriousness of deportment and gratitude of heart, which the recognition of such reiterated and astonishing interpositions of Providence demands of US."

"Divine service is to be performed to-morrow, in the several brigades and divisions."

"We have abundant reasons to thank Providence, for its many favorable interpositions in our behalf. It has, at times, been my only dependence; for, all other resources seemed to have failed us."

"The Great Director of events has carried us through a variety of scenes, during this long and bloody contest, in which we have been, for seven campaigns, most nobly struggling."

"I commend my friends, and, with them, the interests and happiness of our dear country, to the keeping and protection of Almighty God."

"I earnestly pray, that the Omnipotent Being, who has not deserted the cause of America in the hour of its extreme hazard, may never yield so fair a heritage to anarchy or despotism."

"I commend my friends, and, with them, the interests and happiness of our dear country, to the keeping and protection of Almighty God."

"The vicissitudes of war are in the hands of the Supreme Director, where there is no control."

"The propitious smiles of Heaven can never be expected, on a nation that disregards the eternal rules of order and right, which Heaven itself has ordained."

"May we unite, in most humbly offering our prayers and supplications to the Great Lord and Ruler of Nations, and beseech him to pardon our national and other transgressions; ... to render our national government a blessing to all the people, by constantly being a government of wise, just, and constitutional laws, discreetly and faithfully executed and obeyed; to protect and guide. all sovereigns and nations, (especially such as have shown kindness to us), and to bless them with good governments ... as He alone knows to be best."

"I have often expressed my sentiments, that every man, conducting himself as a good citizen, and being accountable to God alone for his religious opinions, ought to be protected, in worshipping the Deity according to the dictates of his own conscience."

"I shall always strive, to prove faithful and impartial patron of genuine, vital religion." (1789)

"It is the duty of all nations, to acknowledge the Providence of Almighty God, to obey his will, to be grateful for his benefits, and humbly to implore his protection and favor."

"It would be peculiarly improper to omit, in this first official act, my fervent supplications to that Almighty Being who rules over the universe, who presides in the councils of nations ... that His benediction may consecrate, to the liberties and happiness of the people of the United States, a government instituted by themselves for these essential purposes ... ."

"No people can be bound to acknowledge and adore the invisible hand which conducts the affairs of men, more than the people of the United States."

"Providence has heretofore taken us up when all other means and hope seemed to be departing from us. In this I will confide."

"The Great Ruler of Events will not permit the happiness of so many millions to be destroyed."

"I humbly implore that Being, on who's Will the fate of nations depends, to crown with success our endeavors ... ."

"Let us unite, in imploring the Supreme Ruler of Nations, to spread his holy protection over these United States; to turn the machinations of the wicked, to the confirming of our Constitution; to enable us, at all times, to root out internal sedition, and put invasion to flight; to perpetuate to our country that prosperity, which His goodness has already conferred, and to verify the anticipations of this government being a safeguard of human rights."

"It is impossible to govern the universe, without the aid of a Supreme Being."

"It is impossible to account for the creation of the universe, without the agency of a Supreme Being."

5

A Christian Young Lady

Writes of Her Father

Eleanor (Nelly) Parke Custis Lewis wrote the letter to follow to Jared Sparks, an author who was at the time compiling a book of the writings of George Washington. He had asked Nelly for information on the religious beliefs of the man who had adopted her. The book was later published as *"The Life of Washington "*.

"Woodlawn, 26 February, 1833.

"Sir,

"I received your favor of the 20th instant last evening, and hasten to give you the information, which you desire.

"Truro Parish is the one in which Mount Vernon, Pohick Church, and Woodlawn are situated. Fairfax Parish is now Alexandria. Before the Federal District was ceded to Congress, Alexandria was in Fairfax County. General Washington had a pew in Pohick Church, and one in Christ Church at Alexandria. He was very instrumental in establishing Pohick Church, and I believe subscribed largely. His pew was near the pulpit. I have a perfect recollection of being there, before his election to the presidency, with him and my grandmother. It was a beautiful church, and had a large, respectable, and wealthy congregation, who were regular attendants.

"He attended the church at Alexandria, when the weather and roads permitted a ride of ten miles. In New York and Philadelphia he never omitted attendance at church in the morning, unless detained by indisposition. The afternoon was spent in his own room at home; the evening with his family, and without company. Sometimes an old and intimate

friend called to see us for an hour or two; but visiting and visitors were prohibited for that day.

"No one in church attended to the services with more reverential respect. My grandmother, who was eminently pious, never deviated from her early habits. She always knelt. The General, as was then the custom, stood during the devotional parts of the service. On communion Sundays, he left the church with me, after the blessing, and returned home, and we sent the carriage back for my grandmother.

"It was his custom to retire to his library at nine or ten o'clock, where he remained an hour before he went to his chamber. He always rose before the sun, and remained in his library until called to breakfasdt [sic]. I never witnessed his private devotions. I never inquired about them. I should have thought it the greatest heresy to doubt his firm belief in Christianity. His life, his writings, prove that he was a Christian. He was not one of those who act or pray, "that they may be seen of men." He communed with his God in secret.

"My mother resided two years at Mount Vernon, after her marriage with John Parke Custis, the only son of Mrs. Washington. I have heard her say that General Washington always received the sacrament with my grandmother before the revolution.

When my aunt, Miss Custis, died suddenly at Mount Vernon, before they could realize the event, he knelt by her and prayed most fervently, most affectingly, for her recovery. Of this I was assured by Judge Washington's mother, and other witnesses.

"He was a silent, thoughtful man. He spoke little generally; never of himself. I never heard him relate a single act of his life during the war I have often seen him perfectly abstracted, his lips moving, but no sound was perceptible. I have sometimes made him laugh most heartily from sympathy with my joyous and extravagant spirits. I was probably one of the last persons on earth to whom he would have addressed serious conversation, particularly when he knew that I had the most perfect model of female excellence ever with me as my monitress, who acted the part of a tender and devoted parent, loving me as only a mother can love, and never extenuating or approving in me what she disapproved in others.

"She never omitted her private devotions, or her public duties; and she and her husband were so perfectly united and happy, that he must have been a Christian. She had no doubts, no fears for him. After forty years of devoted affection and uninterrupted happiness, she resigned him without a murmur into the arms of his Savior and his God, with the assured hope of his eternal felicity. Is it necessary that any one should certify, "General Washington avowed himself to me a believer in Christianity?" As well may we question his patriotism, his heroic, disinterested devotion to his country. His mottos were, *'Deeds, not Words'*; and, *'For God and my Country.'*

"With sentiments of esteem, I am, & c."

6

Prayers of Washington

While a General

And the President

The following prayers are those found in George Washington's personal field notebook. There were a total of 24 pages, each of which was written by this great man. They certainly reveal the depth of his character.

1

Sunday Morning

Almighty God, and most merciful Father, who didst command the children of Israel to offer a daily sacrifice to thee, that thereby they might glorify and praise thee for thy protection both night and day, receive, O Lord, my morning sacrifice which I now offer up to thee; I yield thee humble and hearty thanks that thou has preserved me from the danger of the night past, and brought me to the light of the day, and the comforts thereof, a day which is consecrated to Thine own service and for thine own honor. Let my heart, therefore, Gracious God, be so affected with the glory and majesty of it, that I may not do mine own works, but wait on thee, and discharge those weighty duties thou requirest of me, and since thou art a God of pure eyes, and wilt be sanctified in all who draw near unto thee, who doest not regard the sacrifice of fools, nor hear sinners who tread in thy courts, pardon, I beseech thee, my sins, remove them from thy presence, as far as the east is from the west, and accept of me for the merits of thy son Jesus Christ, that when I come into thy temple, and compass thine altar, my prayers may come before thee as incense; and as thou wouldst hear me calling upon thee in my prayers, so give me grace to hear thee calling on me in thy word, that it may be wisdom, righteousness, reconciliation and peace to the saving of the soul in the day of the Lord Jesus. Grant that I may hear it with reverence, receive it with meekness, mingle it with faith, and that it may accomplish in me, Gracious God, the good work for which thou has sent it. Bless my family, kindred, friends and country, be our God & guide this day and for ever for his sake, who ay down in the Grave and arose again for us, Jesus Christ our Lord, Amen.

2

Sunday Evening

O most Glorious God, in Jesus Christ my merciful and loving father, I acknowledge and confess my guilt, in the weak and imperfect performance of the duties of this day. I have called on thee for pardon and forgiveness of sins, but so coldly and carelessly, that my prayers are become my sin and stand in need of pardon. I have heard thy holy word, but with such deadness of spirit that I have been an unprofitable and forgetful hearer, so that, O Lord, tho' I have done thy work, yet it hath been so negligently that I may rather expect a curse than a blessing from thee. But, O God, who art rich in mercy and plenteous in redemption, mark not, I beseech thee, what I have done amiss; remember that I am but dust, and remit my transgressions, negligences & ignorances, and cover them all with the absolute obedience of thy dear Son, that those sacrifices which I have offered may be accepted by thee, in and for the sacrifice of Jesus Christ offered upon the cross for me; for his sake, ease me of the burden of my sins, and give me grace that by the call of the Gospel I may rise from the slumber of sin into the newness of life. Let me live according to those holy rules which thou hast this day prescribed in thy holy word; make me to know what is acceptable in thy holy word; make me to know what is acceptable in thy sight, and therein to delight, open the eyes of my understanding, and help me thoroughly to examine myself concerning my knowledge, faith and repentance, increase my faith, and direct me to the true object Jesus Christ the way, the truth and the life, bless O Lord, all the people of this land, from the highest to the lowest, particularly those whom thou has appointed to rule over us in church & state. continue thy goodness to me this night. These weak petitions I humbly implore thee to hear accept and ans. for the sake of thy Dear Son Jesus Christ our Lord, Amen.

3

Monday Morning

O eternal and everlasting God, I presume to present myself this morning before thy Divine majesty, beseeching thee to accept of my humble and hearty thanks, that it hath pleased thy great goodness to keep and preserve me the night past from all the dangers poor mortals are subject to, and has given me sweet and pleasant sleep, whereby I find my body refreshed and comforted for performing the duties of this day, in which I beseech thee to defend me from all perils of body and soul. Direct my thoughts, words and work, wash away my sins in the immaculate blood of the lamb, and purge my heart by thy holy spirit, from the dross of my natural corruption, that I may with more freedom of mind and liberty of will serve thee, the ever lasting God, in righteousness and holiness this day, and all the days of my life. Increase my faith in the sweet promises of the gospel; give me repentance from dead works; pardon my wanderings, & direct my thoughts unto thyself, the God of my salvation; teach me how to live in thy fear, labor in thy service, and ever to run in the ways of thy commandments; make me always watchful over my heart, that neither the terrors of conscience, the loathing of holy duties, the love of sin, nor an unwillingness to depart this life, may cast me into a spiritual slumber, but daily frame me more 7 more into the likeness of thy son Jesus Christ, that living in thy fear, and dying in thy favor, I may in thy appointed time attain the resurrection of the just unto eternal life bless my family, friends & kindred unite us all in praising & glorifying thee in all our works begun, continued, and ended, when we shall come to make our last account before thee blessed savior, who hath taught us thus to pray, our Father, & c.

4

Monday Evening

Most Gracious Lord God, from whom proceedeth every good and perfect gift, I offer to thy divine majesty my unfeigned praise & thanksgiving for all thy mercies towards me. Thou mad'st me at first and hast ever since sustained the work of thy own hand; thou gav'st thy Son to die for me; and hast given me assurance of salvation, upon my repentance and sincerely endeavoring to conform my life to his holy precepts and example. Thou art pleased to lengthen out to me the time of repentance and to move me to it by thy spirit and by the word, by thy mercies, and by thy judgments; out of a deepness of thy mercies, and by my own unworthiness, I do appear before thee at this time; I have sinned and done very wickedly, be merciful to me, O God, and pardon me for Jesus Christ sake; instruct me in the particulars of my duty, and suffer me not to be tempted above what thou givest me strength to bear. Take care, I pray thee of my affairs and more and more direct me in thy truth, defend me from my enemies, especially my spiritual ones. Suffer me not to be drawn from thee, by the blandishments of the world, carnal desires, the cunning of the devil, or deceitfulness of sin. work in me thy good will and pleasure, and discharge my mind from all things that are displeasing to thee, of all ill will and discontent, wrath and bitterness, pride & vain conceit of myself, and render me charitable, pure, holy, patient and heavenly minded. be with me at the hour of death; dispose me for it, and deliver me from the slavish fear of it, and make me willing and fit to die whenever thou shalt call me hence. Bless our rulers in church and state. bless O Lord the whole race of mankind, and let the world be filled with the knowledge of Thee and thy son Jesus Christ. Pity the sick, the poor, the weak, the needy, the widows and fatherless, and all that morn or are broken in heart, and be merciful to them according to their several necessities. bless my friends and grant me grace to forgive my enemies as heartily as I desire forgiveness of Thee my heavenly Father. I beseech thee to defend me this night from all evil, and do more for me than I can think or ask, for Jesus Christ sake, in whose most holy name & words, I continue to pray, Our Father, & c.

5

Tuesday Morning

O Lord our God, most mighty and merciful father, I thine unworthy creature and servant, do once more approach thy presence. Though not worthy to appear before thee, because of my natural corruptions, and the many sins and transgressions which I have committed against thy divine majesty; yet I beseech thee, for the sake of him in whom thou art well pleased, the Lord Jesus Christ, to admit me to render thee deserved thanks and praises for thy manifold mercies extended toward me, for the quiet rest & repose of the past night, for food, rainment, health, peace, liberty, and the hopes of a better life through the merits of thy dear son's bitter passion. and O kind father continue thy mercy and favor to me this day, and ever hereafter; propose all my lawful undertakings; et me have all my directions from thy holy spirit; and success from thy bountiful hand. Let the bright beams of thy light so shine into my heart, and enlighten my mind in understanding thy blessed word, that I may be enabled to perform thy will in all things, and effectually resist all temptations of the world, the flesh and the devil. preserve and defend our rulers in church & state. bless the people of this land, be a father to the fatherless, a comforter to the comfortless, a deliverer to the captives, and a physician to the sick. Let thy blessings guide this day and forever through J. C. in whose blessed form of prayer I conclude my weak petitions--Our Father, & c.

6

Tuesday Evening

Most gracious God and heavenly father, we cannot cease, but must cry unto thee for mercy, because my sins cry against me for justice. How shall I address myself unto thee, I must with the publican stand and admire at thy great goodness, tender mercy, and long suffering towards me, in that thou hast kept me the past day from being consumed and brought to naught. O Lord, what is man, or the son of man, that thou regardest him; the more days pass over my head, the more sins and iniquities I heap up against thee. If I should cast up the account of my good deeds done this day, how few and small would they be; but if I should reckon my miscarriages, surely they would be many and great. O, blessed father, let thy son's blood wash me from all impurities, and cleanse me from the stains of sin that are upon me. Give me grace to lay hold upon his merits; that they may be my reconciliation and atonement unto thee,--That I may know my sins are forgiven by his death & passion. embrace me in the arms of thy mercy; vouchsafe to receive me unto the bosom of thy love, shadow me with thy wings, that I may safely rest under thy suspicion this night; and so into thy hands I commend myself, both soul and body, in the name of thy son, J. C., beseeching Thee, when this life shall end, I may take my everlasting rest with thee in thy heavenly kingdom. bless all in authority over us, be merciful to all those afflicted with thy cross or calamity, bless all my friends, forgive my enemies and accept my thanksgiving this evening for all the mercies and favors afforded me; hear and graciously answer these my requests, and whatever else thou see'st needful grant us, for the sake of Jesus Christ in whose blessed name and words I continue to pray, Our Father, & c.

7

A Prayer for Wednesday Morning

Almighty and eternal Lord God, the great creator of heaven & earth, and the God and Father of our Lord Jesus Christ; look down from heaven, in pity and compassion upon me thy servant, who humbly prostrate myself before thee, sensible of thy mercy and my own misery; there is an infinite distance between thy glorious majesty and me, thy poor creature, the work of thy hand, between thy infinite power, and my weakness, thy wisdom, and my folly, thy eternal Being, and my mortal frame, but, O Lord, I have set myself at a greater distance from thee by my sin and wickedness, and humbly acknowledge the corruption of my nature and the many rebellions of my life. I have sinned against heaven and before thee, in thought, word & deed; I have contemned thy majesty and holy laws. I have likewise sinned by omitting what I ought to do, and committing what I ought not. I have rebelled against light, despised thy mercies and judgments, and broken my vows and promises; I have neglected the means of Grace, and opportunities of becoming better; my iniquities are multiplies, and my sins are very great. I confess them, O Lord, with shame and sorrow, detestation and loathing, and desire to be vile in my own eyes, as I have rendered myself vile in thine. I humbly beseech thee to be merciful to me in the free pardon of my sins, for the sake of thy dear Son, my only savior, J. C., who came not to call the righteous, but sinners to repentance; be pleased to renew my nature and write thy laws upon my heart, and help me to live, righteously, soberly, and godly in this evil worlds; make me humble, meek, patient and contented, and work in me the grace of thy holy spirit. Prepare me for death and judgment, and let the thoughts thereof awaken me to a greater care and study to approve myself unto thee in well doing. bless our rulers in church & state. Help all in affliction or adversity--give them patience and a sanctified use of their affliction, and in thy good time deliverance from them; forgive my enemies, take me unto thy protection this day, keep me in perfect peace, which I ask in the name & for the sake of Jesus. Amen.

8

Wednesday Evening

Holy and eternal Lord God who art the King of heaven, and the watchman of Israel, that never slumberest or sleepest, what shall we render unto thee for all thy benefits; because thou hast inclined thine ears unto me, therefore will I call on thee as long as I live, from the rising of the sun to the going down of the same let thy name be praised. among the infinite riches of thy mercy towards me, I desire to render thanks & praise for thy merciful preservation of me this day, as well as all the days of my life; and for the many other blessings & mercies spiritual & temporal which thou hast bestowed on me, contrary to my deserving. All these thy mercies call on me to be thankful and my infirmities & wants call for a continuance of thy tender mercies; cleanse my soul, O Lord, I beseech thee, from whatever is offensive to thee, and hurtful to me, and give me what is convenient for me. watch over me this night, and give me comfortable and sweet sleep to fit me for the service of the day following. Let my soul watch for the coming of the Lord Jesus; let my bed put me in mind of my grave, and my rising from there of my last resurrection; O heavenly Father, so frame this heart of mine, that I may ever delight to live according to thy will and command, in holiness and righteousness before thee all the days of my life. Let me remember, O Lord, the time will come when the trumpet shall sound, and the dead shall rise and stand before the judgment seat, and give an account of whatever they have done in the body, and let me so prepare my soul, that I may do it with joy and not with grief. bless the rulers and people of this and forget not those who are under any affliction or oppression. Let thy favor be extended to all my relations friends and all others who I ought to remember in my prayer and hear me I beseech thee for the sake of my dear redeemer in whose most holy words, I farther pray, Our Father, & c.

9

Thursday Morning

Most gracious Lord God, whose dwelling is in the highest heavens, and yet beholdest the lowly and humble upon the earth, I blush and am ashamed to lift up my eyes to thy dwelling place, because I have sinned against thee; look down, I beseech thee upon me thy unworthy servant who prostrate myself at the footstool of thy mercy, confessing my own guiltiness, and begging pardon for my sins; what couldst thou have done Lord more for me, or what could I have done more against thee? Thou didst send me thy Son to take nature upon.

NOTE: The prayer book ended on this page. Were the rest of Washington's prayer pages lost? Or did he not complete his prayer list? This has never been determined.

Other Prayers of Washington
Washington's Prayer on May 1, 1777, when he received the news that France was joining the Colonies in the War for American Independence:

"And now, Almighty Father, if it is Thy holy will that we shall obtain a place and name among the nations of the earth, grant that we may be enabled to show our gratitude for Thy goodness by our endeavors to fear and obey Thee. Bless us with Thy wisdom in our counsels, success in battle, and let all our victories be tempered with humanity. Endow, also, our enemies with enlightened minds, that they become sensible of their injustice, and willing to restore our liberty and peace. Grant the petition of Thy servant, for the sake of Him whom Thou hast called Thy beloved Son; nevertheless, not my will, but Thine be done."

Washington's Prayer

Washington's Prayer has been preserved for posterity on the plaque at Pohick Church in Fairfax, Virginia. Washington was a vestryman there from 1762 to 1784. It is also to be found on a plaque in New York City's St. Paul's Chapel:

"Almighty God; We make our earnest prayer that Thou wilt keep the United States in Thy Holy protection; and Thou wilt incline the hearts of the Citizens to cultivate a spirit of subordination and obedience to Government; and entertain a brotherly affection and love for one(another and for their fellow Citizens of the United States at large, and particularly for their brethren who have served in

the Field.

"And finally that Thou wilt most graciously be pleased to dispose us all to do justice, to love mercy, and to demean ourselves with that Charity, humility, and pacific temper of mind which were the Characteristics of the Divine Author of our blessed Religion, and without a humble imitation of whose example in these things we can never hope to be a happy nation.

"Grant our supplication, we beseech Thee, through Jesus Christ our Lord. Amen."

7

Washington's Astounding

Prophetic Dream

Washington's Headquarters at Valley Forge where the "vision" is said to have taken place.

Martha spent her days with her husband at Valley Forge. The slept in the upstairs bedroom to the left of the stairs. The standing rule was that no one, *absolutely no one*, was to disturb them while they were having breakfast up there.

The Dire Situation Faced in 1777

One of the most significant events in the life of this *Man of Destiny* will not be found in any of our high school or college history texts. But it most certainly should be!

It is said to have taken place during the dread winter of 1777. This was a tie when the War for Independence wasn't going very well for the vastly outnumbered and ill-equipped Colonial forces. This was a time when the Revolutionary War wasn't going at all well for the vastly outnumbered and ill-equipped Colonial forces.

John Grady, M.D., historian from Benton, Tennessee, lucidly describes circumstances: *"The winter at Valley Forge was bitter cold. The Continental Army under General George Washington had little food, inadequate shelter, and insufficient clothing. Many soldiers had no boots – their bloody feet were wrapped in rags. Often there was no pay. Sickness ravaged the camp. Before spring, more than one third of the men would die of disease or desert the cause. All odds were against them. ..."*

The Continental Army had been defeated in two major battles and British invaders occupied Philadelphia!

The British Army had forced Washington to retreat to the Pennsylvania plains!

Things certainly weren't looking good for the Colonial forces!

It was a time of desperation!

The situation couldn't have been more precarious!

There was little or no hope for victory!

Famine was at the door step!

It was constantly very, very cold!

The temperature often fell well below zero!

Gale like winds blew throughout the encampment!

Shoeless soldiers struggled through the icy slush and snow!

Foot prints in blood could be readily seen on the snow covered ground!

Feet and legs had to be amputated after freezing and turning black!

There was a shortage of blankets and the men had none to wrap themselves in when trying to sleep.

What tattered clothing there was didn't come close to covering their bodies!

Morale was for all practical purposes non-existent. It was at an all time low!

More than 3,000 patriots died that winter.

Nor did many have clothing to cover their bare bodies.

American forces were desperately fighting against the British, at the time the most powerful and well armed nation in the world!

Defeat stared Washington in the face!

There was no hope for victory that day during the winter of 1777!

Surrender appeared to be inevitable!

The General gathered his weary troops around him on Christmas Eve and read them the inspiring immortal words of Thomas Paine: *"These are the times that try men's souls. The summer soldier and the sunshine patriot will, in this crisis, shrink from the service of their country: but he that stands it now, deserves the love and thanks of man and woman. Tyranny, like hell, is not easily conquered; yet we have this consolation with us, that the harder the conflict, the more glorious the triumph. What we obtain too cheap, we esteem too lightly: it is dearness only that gives everything its value. Heaven knows how to put a proper price upon goods; and it would be strange indeed if so celestial an article as freedom should not be so highly rated".*

Washington's men were mightily inspired after listening to the deeply moving words of Paine.

They were further strengthened by the strong, unrelenting determination of their leader. He inspired his troops on to victory when he told them this: *"The time is now near at hand which must probably determine whether Americans are to be freemen or slaves; whether they are to have any property they can call their own; whether their houses and farms are to be pillaged and destroyed, and themselves consigned to a state of wretchedness from which no human efforts will deliver them.*

"The fate of unborn millions will now depend, under God , on the courage of this army. Our cruel and unrelenting enemy leaves us only the choice of brave resistance, or the most abject submission. We have, therefore to resolve to conquer or die."

The loyal men at Valley Forge were deeply encouraged. They were now much more highly motivated. And they were confident in the providence of God. They reassembled in a fighting mood, crossed the icy Delaware River, and won the battle of Trenton. This was the turning point in the Revolutionary War.

Despite all of the insurmountable conditions, did God chose this time of wretched misery, this time of despair and bleak gloominess, to pay a visit to Washington in a dream? To reveal to him a vision through an angelic visitor as in the days of old?

Perhaps.

Nevertheless, a great number of people do believe that God chose this time during the dread winter of 1777, to give a prophetic vision to George Washington.

The story of this remarkable event is fully covered below.

Setting the Scene

Did it happen that the great General momentarily dozed and dreamed while sitting in his headquarters at Valley Forge? Or did he have an angelic visit through a daydream?

This is the time when George Washington is  purported to have had a vision that described the future of the Republic -- included were victory in the Revolutionary War; the fighting between Americans in a Civil War; and a World War yet to come.

Yet, great caution must be taken in the acceptance of the validity of any visions or dreams of men. Washington's purported vision, does however, have some quite remarkable factors which seem to be fully factual with regards to U.S. history.

The Origination of the Story

The story of Washington's purported *"vision"* was in the beginning published in the **NATIONAL TRIBUNE** in 1859 and subsequently reprinted in other publications including **THE STARS AND**

STRIPES.   The *"vision"* was initially described to a reporter named Wesley Bradshaw by an officer (Anthony Sherman) who claims to have served under General Washington at Valley Forge during the winter of 1777.

How it All Began

Mr. Bradshaw begins: *"The last time I ever saw Anthony Sherman was on the Fourth of July, 1859, in Independence Square. He was then 99 years old, and becoming very feeble. But though so old, his dimming eyes rekindled as he gazed upon Independence Hall, which he had come to visit once more."*

"Let's go into the hall," said Mr. Sherman. *"I want to tell you of an incident of Washington's life, one which no one alive knows of except myself; and if you live, you will before long see it verified. Mark the prediction, you will see it verified."*

Washington's Vision
As Related by Anthony Sherman

"From the opening of the Revolution we experienced all phases of fortune," reveals Mr. Sherman, *" now good and now ill, one time victorious and another conquered. The darkest period we had, I*

think, was when Washington after several reverses, retreated to Valley Forge, where he resolved to pass the winter of 1777.

"Ah! I have often seen the tears coursing down our dear commander's care-worn cheeks, as he would be conversing with a confidential officer about the condition of his poor soldiers. You have doubtless heard the story of Washington's going to  the thicket to pray. Well, it was not only true, but he used often to pray in secret for aid and comfort. And God brought us safely through the darkest days of tribulation.

"One day, I remember it well, the chilly winds whistled through the leafless trees, though the sky was cloudless and the sun shone brightly. He remained in his quarters nearly all the afternoon, alone. When he came out I noticed that his face was a shade paler than usual, and there seemed to be something on his mind of more than ordinary importance. Returning just after dark, he dispatched an orderly to the quarters of an office, who was presently in attendance. After a preliminary conversation of about half an hour, Washington, gazing upon his companion with *that strange look of dignity which he alone could command, said to the latter:*

WASHINGTON DESCRIBES HIS GUESTS

"I do not know whether it is going to the anxiety of my mind, or what, but this afternoon, as I was sitting at this table engaged in preparing a dispatch, something in the apartment seemed to disturb me. Looking up, I beheld standing opposite me a singularly beautiful being. So astonished was I, for I had given strict orders not to be disturbed that it was some moments before I found language to inquire the cause of the visit. A second, a third, and even a fourth time did I repeat the question, but received no answer from my mysterious visitor except a slight raising of the eyes.

"By this time I felt strange sensations spreading over me. I would have risen but the riveted gaze of the being before me rendered volition impossible. I assayed once more to speak, but my tongue had become useless, as if paralyzed. A new influence, mysterious, potent, irresistible, took possession of me. All I could do was to gaze steadily, vacantly at my unknown visitor.

"Gradually the surrounding atmosphere seemed to fill with sensation, and grew luminous.

Everything about me seemed to rarefy, the mysterious visitor also becoming more airy and yet more distinct to my eyes than before. I began to feel as one dying, or rather to experience the sensations which I have sometimes imagined accompanied death. I did not think, I did not reason, I did not move. All were alike impossible. I was only conscious of gazing fixedly, vacantly, at my companion.

THE DEFEAT OF THE BRITISH FORETOLD?

"Presently I heard a voice saying, **'Son of the Republic, look and learn,'** *while at the same time my visitor extended an arm eastward.*

"I now beheld a heavy white vapor at some distance rising fold upon fold. This gradually dissipated, and I looked upon a strange scene. Before me lay, spread out in one vast plain, all the countries of the world, Europe, Asia, Africa, and America. I saw rolling and tossing between Europe and America the billows of the Atlantic, and between Asia and America lay the Pacific.

"'Son of the Republic,' said the same mysterious voice as before, 'look and learn.'

"At that moment I beheld a dark, shadowy being, like an angel, standing, or rather floating in

107

mid-air, between Europe and America. Dipping water out of the ocean in the hollow of each hand, he sprinkled some upon America with his right hand, while with his left he cast some over Europe. Immediately a cloud arose from these countries, and joined in mid ocean. For awhile it seemed stationary, and then it moved slowly westward, until it enveloped America in its murky folds. Sharp flashes of lightening gleamed through it at intervals, and I heard the smothered groans and cries of the American people.

"A second time the angel dipped from the ocean and sprinkled it out as before. The dark cloud was then drawn back to the ocean, in whose billows it sank from view.

THE CIVIL WAR PREDICTED?

"A third time I heard the mysterious visitor saying, **'Son of the Republic, look and learn.'**

" I cast my eyes upon America and beheld villages and towns and cities springing up one after another until the whole land from the Atlantic to the Pacific was dotted with them. Again, I heard the mysterious voice say, **'Son of the Republic, the end of the century cometh, look and learn.'**

*"And this time the dark shadowy angel turned his face southward. From Africa I saw an ill-omened specter approach our land. It flitted slowly and heavily over every town and city of the latter. The inhabitants presently set themselves in battle array against each other. As I continued looking, I saw a bright angel on whose brow rested a crown of light, on which was traced the word **'Union.'** He was bearing the American flag. He placed the flag between the divided nation and said, **'remember, ye are brethren.'***

THE NORTH AND SOUTH REUNITE?

"Instantly, the inhabitants, casting down their weapons, became friends once more and united around the National Standard.

WORLD WAR III PRESAGED?

*"Again, I heard the mysterious voice saying, **'Son of the republic, look and learn.'** At this the dark, shadowy angel placed a trumpet to his mouth, and blew three distinct blasts; and taking water from the ocean, he sprinkled it upon Europe, Asia, and Africa.*

"Then my eyes beheld a fearful scene. From each of these continents arose thick black clouds that were soon joined into one. And through this mass

there gleamed a dark red light by which I saw hordes of armed men. These men, moving with the cloud, marched by land and sailed by sea to America, which country was enveloped in the volume of the cloud. And I dimly saw these vast armies devastate the whole country and burn the villages, towns and cities which I had seen springing up.

*"As my ears listened to the thundering of the cannon, clashing of swords, and the shouts and cries of millions in mortal combat, I again heard the mysterious voice saying, **'Son of the Republic, look and learn.'** When this voice had ceased, the dark shadowy angel placed his trumpet once more to his mouth, and blew a long and fearful blast.*

GOD TO COME TO THE AID OF AMERICA?

*"Instantly a light as of a thousand suns shone down from above me, and pierced and broke into fragments the dark cloud which enveloped America. At the same moment the angel upon whose head still shown the word **'Union'** and who bore our national flag in one hand and a sword in the other, descended from the heavens attended by legions of white spirits. these immediately joined the inhabitants of America, who I perceived were well-nigh overcome, but who immediately taking courage again, closed up their broken ranks and renewed the battle.*

*"Again, amid the fearful noise of the conflict I heard the mysterious voice saying, **'Son of the Republic, look and learn.'** As the voice ceased, the shadowy angel for the last time dipped water from the ocean and sprinkled it upon America. Instantly the dark cloud rolled back, together with the armies it had brought, leaving the inhabitants of the land victorious.*

AMERICA'S DESTINY REVEALED?

*"Then once more, I beheld the villages, towns, and cities springing up where I had seen them before, while the bright angel, planting the azure standard he had brought in the midst of them, cried with a loud voice: **'While the stars remain, and the heavens send down dew upon the earth, so long shall the Union last.'** And taking from his brow the crown on which blazoned the word **'Union'** he placed it upon the standard while the people kneeling down said, **'amen.'***

*"The scene instantly began to fade and dissolve, and I at last saw nothing but the rising, curling vapor I at first beheld. This also disappeared, and I found myself once more gazing upon the mysterious visitor, who, in the same voice I had heard before, said, **'Son of the Republic, what you have seen is thus interpreted. Three great perils will come***

upon the Republic. The most fearful for her is the third. But the whole world united shall not prevail against her. let every child of the Republic learn to live for his God, his land and Union.'

"With these words the vision vanished, and I started from my seat and felt that I had seen a vision wherein had been shown me the birth, the progress, and the destiny of the United States."

"Such, my friend," the venerable narrator, Anthony Sherman, concluded, *"were the words I heard from Washington's own lips, and America will do well to profit by them."*

Pros and Cons
What Do You Think?

According to one obscure internet source: *"This story, charming as it is, appears to be an old hoax. There is no record of Washington ever relating a tale of such a vision* (not according to Anthony Sherman). *The story surfaced long after his death."* What difference could this possibly make insofar as ascertaining its authenticity?

Furthermore, this same source reports the following; *"Oddly enough, the park rangers at Valley*

Forge are now forbidden to acknowledge George Washington's words."

Even if it's true that the park rangers at Valley Forge aren't allowed to discuss the subject, this doesn't mean that the story as related by Mr. Sherman is proven false. It simply means that it can't be verified other than by the word of one man. And therefore, it can't be officially acknowledged as historically accurate beyond question. This is completely understandable.

In an apparent effort to diffuse any real likelihood that Washington could possibly have had such an astounding vision in a dream, the Independence Hall Association says this: *"Washington, while willing to refer to religion in political speeches, was not himself a religious man."*

Not a religious man? Literally hundreds of other sources indicate otherwise. His own words for example. Many of his contemporaries also speak of Washington's faith. Read his daughter's letter regarding her gather and his religious beliefs and practices in Chapter 4.

The same source unequivocally declares: *"Despite the story being a fraud, it is an old fraud and an historically significant one."*

Yet, they offer nothing further to substantiate their charge of *"fraud."*

Why?

Because there is absolutely nothing to support such a conclusion!

Some people will say that General Washington's vision is validated by the fact that a copy of the account is in the Library of Congress. This argument of authenticity is misleading in and of itself. The Library of Congress has copies of *anything* and everything published in America. This *doesn't* in any manner indicate truthfulness of the content.

I'm not aware of any eighteenth-century evidence that corroborates this story. The soldier mentioned as having a first-hand account of the *"Vision,"* Anthony Sherman, *was* a soldier in the Continental Army. However, according to his pension application, he was at Saratoga under the command of Benedict Arnold at the end of 1777. He is believed to have joined the main forces in 1778 just before the Battle of Monmouth, New Jersey.

Nevertheless, Dr. John Grady, nationally known author, speaker, and patriot, as well as being my friend, offers this:

"As the prophets of old were shown the destiny of mankind, so was Washington shown the destiny of our nation.

"God molded, inspired and directed George Washington.

"He was, indeed, chosen to be a special man,
"At a special time,
"For a special purpose."

8

The Validity

of

Prophetic Dreams

Throughout History

The *Bible* is filled with a multitude of excellent dream data -- both in the *Old* and the *New Testaments.* Throughout the entire Bible there is abundant evidence of a belief in the supernatural origin of dreams. It was an accepted and honored means of communication between the Deity and his chosen ones, for it is written: *"I will pour out my Spirit upon all flesh; and your sons and daughters shall prophesy, your old men shall dream dreams, and your young men shall see visions."*

The best-known dreams of the Old Testament are those of Daniel, Jacob, and Joseph. Some authorities claim that the Book of Daniel was written from a dream.

The *Book of Daniel* contains a number of prophetic dreams which were fulfilled to the letter:

The insanity of Nebuchadnezzar and his downfall were presaged.

So was the eventual overthrow of the despotic Balthazar.

Jacob was a man who had many dreams. His dream of the celestial ladder uniting heaven and earth constitutes one of the most beautiful passages in *Genesis.*

His father-in-law, Laban, was warned in a dream that he must not harm Jacob.

In another instance, a distressed King Saul cries out, *"God is departed from me, and answereth me no more, neither by prophets, nor by dreams."*

Joseph, the son of Jacob, was widely known as the "dreamer." While he was in Egypt and working for the pharaoh, the Egyptian monarch had the famous prophetic dream of the fat and lean cattle. Joseph interpreted this dream as a warning of a coming famine. He said: *"God hath shewed pharaoh what he is about to do."*

This dream is credited with saving Egypt from famine and Joseph was aptly rewarded by being appointed chief advisor to the king. The birth of Jesus Christ was also foretold to Joseph in one of his many dreams.

Dreams play a major role as warnings throughout the *New Testament*:

The Holy Family was advised in a dream to go into Egypt.

Pontius Pilate's wife warned him after she had a vivid dream at the time of the crucifixion: *"Have thou nothing to do with that just man: for I have suffered many things this day in a dream because of him!"*

Paul was a man who dreamed with regularity.

Many of the apostles were initially converted to Christianity after experiencing dreams.

A multitude of subsequent saints were strongly influenced by dreams—among them is St. Augustine.

Rome's most educated citizens, as well as

those of Athens, devoted much time to contemplating and then writing about dreams. These included such notables as Socrates and Plato.

Plato contended that there were divine manifestations to the soul during sleep.

Dreams are ascribed a supernatural origin by Homer, and in the Greek and Roman classics are numerous descriptions of unusual prophetic dreams.

Many kings and queens have been given warnings of impending danger through a dream:

Caesar, on the night before he was murdered, continually had the same dream. He saw himself *"soaring above the clouds on wings."* And he saw himself placing his *"hand within the right hand of Jove."*

Caesar's wife also tried to warn him on the impending danger. She, too, had experienced a terrible dream the evening prior to his assassination.

Cassius of Parma, a supporter of Mark Anthony in a political power struggle, fled Rome and hid in Athens after the difficult battle of Actium. He was sleeping one night and dreamed of a tall, heavy-set, dark man who snarled: *"I am your evil genius."* The ghastly apparition appeared again and again in his dreams, always saying exactly the same thing. Cassius was frightened, but never fully realized the warning he was being given. Early the next morning, he was brutally murdered by order of Emperor Augustus.

Cicero writes of two traveling Acadians who

visited the city of Megara. One went to stay with friends, the other got a room at a local inn. The man who lodged with his friends had a shattering dream that his traveling companion was calling out to him for assistance. The innkeeper was going to kill the man. The dreamer awoke in a sweat, brushed off the horrible dream as nonsense, and proceeded to go back to sleep.

His friend at the inn appeared in still another dream, this time to tell him it was now too late. He said he had already been murdered, his body tossed in a wooden cart, and covered with dung. Lastly, he revealed that his murderer would try to sneak his body out of town the very next morning. The dreamer now quickly got up, went to see the local authorities, and had the cart searched. The dead body of his friend was easily located and the killer was brought to justice.

The Emperor Marcian dreamed that he saw the bow of the Hunnish conqueror break. This took place on the same night Attila met his death.

Plutarch reveals how Augustus, while sick, was persuaded he should leave his tent after being told of a dream's prophetic warning by a close friend. A few short hours later, his enemies moved in and the bed on which Augustus had slept was pierced by many swords. Heeding a friend's dream saved this leader's life.

Croesus witnessed his son being killed in a dream. And Petrarch clearly talked to his beloved

Laura in a dream on the day she died. This dream was the inspiration for his lovely poem, *"The Triumph of Death."*

And even Joan of Arc presaged her own death in one of her dreams.

The distinguished violinist, Tartini, composed the *Devil's Sonata* after having a most unusual dream. According to Tartini, he was challenged to a contest of playing skills while having a dream. When he awoke, the music was burned into his mind. He easily committed the entire composition to paper.

President Abraham Lincoln and his wife were spending part of a quiet afternoon visiting with friends in the White House. It was Good Friday, April 14, 1865. He described a haunting dream he had recently experienced:

"About ten days ago I retired very late. . . I soon began to dream. There seemed to be a deathlike stillness about me. Then I heard subdued sobs as if a number of people were weeping. I thought I had left my bed and wandered downstairs. There the silence was broken by the same pitiful sobbing, but the mourners were invisible. I went from room to room. No living person was in sight, but the same mournful sounds of distress met me as I passed along. Every object was familiar to me, but nowhere could I see the people who were grieving as though their hearts would break. I was puzzled and alarmed.

Determined to find the cause of a state of things so mysterious and so shocking, I kept on until I arrived at the East Room. There I met with a sickening surprise. Before me was a catafalque, on which rested a corpse wrapped in funeral vestments. Around it were stationed soldiers who were acting as guards; and there was a throng of people, some gazing mournfully at the corpse, whose face was covered, others weeping pitifully.

"Who is dead in the White House? I demanded of one of the soldiers.

"The President, was his answer. He was killed by an assassin.

"Then came a loud burst of grief from the crowd, which awoke me from my dream. It is only a dream but it has strangely annoyed me, however. Let us say no more about it."

That very evening, while sitting in the State Box at Ford's Theater, attending the evening performance of ***"Our American Cousin,"*** the President was shot by John Wilkes Booth. He died the next day, April 15, 1865

9

Biographical Sketches

Of

Washington's Better Known

Contemporaries

John Adams
(1735 – 1826)

Heritage: English. Born in Braintree (now Quincy), Massachusetts. Direct descendant of John Alden who came to America on the Mayflower

Religion: Christian. Considered going into the ministry. He said this: *"The Ten Commandments and the Sermon on the Mount contain my religion"*

Education: Graduated from Harvard College in 1775. Later studied law.

Marriage: Married Abigail Smith on October 26, 1764, when she was 20. From a Christian family, both her father and grandfather were clergymen.

Children: Four children – three sons and a daughter.

Interesting Highlights: Delegate to the Continental Congress from 1774 to 1778.

He and his cousin, Samuel Adams, were two of the 49 men who signed the *Declaration of Independence* on August 2, 1776. Six others signed the *Declaration* at a later date. They were Gerry, Richard Henry Lee, McKean, Thornton, Wolcott and Wythe. John Hancock was *only* man to sign on July 4.

He and Abigail's life together was one of history's everlasting love affairs.

A major force behind getting the various states to ratify the *Constitution.*

John Adams and Jefferson (1743-1826) were two of the last three Signers of the *Declaration of Independence* to die. Charles Carroll (1737-1832) was the last.

America's second President (1797-1801) following George Washington.

Most influential in getting Washington appointed as Commander-in-Chief of the Continental Army.

Quotable Quote: When the Continental Congress approved the *Declaration,* he said: *"It ought to be commemorated, as a Day of deliverance, by solemn acts of devotion to God Almighty."*

Heroic Deed: Signing the *Declaration.* John Adams knew that should the struggle for Independence fail, an ignominious death by hanging would most certainly be his punishment.

Refused offer of amnesty from British Governor Gage in June 1775.

Little Known Fact: Worked with Franklin and Jefferson on a special committee to develop the *Declaration of Independence.*

Price Paid for Signing: Especially high price put on his head. He eluded capture, even though the British hunted him down like an animal. All the Signers, including Adams, suffered monetary losses because of their connection with the cause. Some were brought to the brink of financial ruin, or even worse, abject poverty.

John Hancock
(1737 – 1793)

Heritage: Born near Quincy, Massachusetts. Descendant of an English family who immigrated to America sometime in the late 1600s or early 1700s.

Religion: Devout Christian. Father and grandfather were Congregational ministers of note in Massachusetts. See quote below.

Education: Had only the finest tutors. Studied at the prestigious Boston Latin School. Graduated from Harvard College when 17 in 1754

Marriage: Married beautiful Dorothy Quincy on August 23, 1775. She was a relative of John and Samuel Adams. He was 38, she 28.

Children: Two. Daughter died as an infant and a son, John George Washington Hancock, died when 9 years old.

Interesting Highlights: Delegate to the First Continental Congress that convened on September 5, 1774, at Carpenter's Hall in Philadelphia.

President of the Second Continental Congress that convened on May 10, 1775, at the State House in Philadelphia.

His wife, Dorothy, also an ardent patriot.

Dorothy's father, Judge Quincy, also a fearless patriot, strongly supported his son-in-laws fight for American independence.

Only man to actually affix his signature on the *Declaration of Independence,* July 4, 1776. There were 49 others who signed on August 2, 1776. Six signed at a later date – Gerry, Richard Henry Lee, McKean, Thornton, Wolcott and Wythe.

Boldly stepped forward, picked up the quill, and placed his name on the Declaration in large letters. Stepping back, he spoke those immortal words: *"There! His Majesty can now read my name without spectacles, and can now double his reward of 500 pounds on my head. That is my defiance."*

Quotable Quote: *"We think it is incumbent upon this people to humble themselves before God on account of their sins. ... so God may be pleased to continue to us the blessings we enjoy, and remove the tokens of His displeasure."* Spoken on the eve of the Revolution (October 1774).

Heroic Deed: Signing the *Declaration*. John Hancock knew that should the struggle for independence fail, an ignominious death by hanging would most certainly be his punishment.

Refused an offer of amnesty from British Governor Gage in June 1775.

Little Known Fact: As a Major General in the Massachusetts militia, he led an expeditionary force to oust the British from Rhode Island.

Punishment: All the Signers, including Hancock, suffered monetary losses because of their connection with the cause. Some were brought to the brink of financial ruin, or even worse, abject poverty.

Charles Carroll
(1737 – 1832)

Heritage: Irish descent. Grandfather, Daniel, emigrated from Ireland to America toward the end of the 17th Century.

Religion: Christian. A leader in Maryland's Catholic community.

Education: Taken to France when 8-years old (1745) to attend a Jesuit college in St. Omers. More education followed in Paris and London until he graduated. Studied law in London.

Marriage: Married distant cousin, Mary Darnell, on June 5, 1768. He was 31, she was 21. Mary died at age 35 in 1782. Charles never remarried.

Children: Six daughters, one son. Four daughters died as infants or in early childhood. Children who lived were Mary, born in 1770; Charles born in 1775; and Catherine, born in 1778.

Interesting Highlights: One of 56 men to sign the *Declaration of Independence*. Hancock was the *only* one to sign on July 4, 1776. Another 49 signed on August 2. Six signed at a later date – they were Richard Henry Lee, Gerry, McKean, Thorton, Wolcott and Wythe.

The only Roman Catholic to sign the *Declaration of Independence*.

Believed to be one of the wealthiest man in America when he died.

Passage of the ***Stamp Act*** in 1765 arrested his attention. Immediately supported the patriot cause. At this time he became closely associated with numerous future Signers of the *Declaration* including Chase, Paca, Stone.

Appointed in 1776 to be a delegate to the convention that framed a *Constitution* for Maryland as an independent State.

Last survivor of the 56 who signed the *Declaration of Independence*.

Quotable Quote: B. J. Lansing said this: " *...he was the last vestige that remained upon earth of that holy brotherhood, who stood sponsor at the baptism in blood of our infant republic.* "

Heroic Deed: Signing the *Declaration of Independence*. Charles Carroll knew that should the struggle for independence fail, an ignominious death by hanging would most certainly be his punishment.

Refused offer of amnesty from British Governor Gage in June 1775.

Little Known Fact: One of America's largest landowners, Hancock asked if he would sign the *Declaration*. Carroll responded: *"Most assuredly."* When finished, he stepped back and said: *"Well, there go a few thousand."*

Price Paid for Signing: All the Signers, including Carroll, suffered monetary losses because of their connection with the cause. Some were brought to the brink of financial ruin, or even worse, abject poverty.

Benjamin Franklin
(1706 – 1790)

Heritage: English. Born in Boston. Father immigrated in 1682 to America from England and settled in Massachusetts.

Religion: Christian. A Puritan. Franklin said this on the eve of the American War for Independence in 1774: *"We think it is incumbent upon this people to humble themselves before God on account of their sins."*

Education: Could never afford private tutoring or prestigious schools. Read and studied on his own extensively. Taught himself five languages.

Marriage: Took a common law wife in September of 1730. She was Deborah Read, a 25-year old Philadelphia widow. Franklin was 24 at the time. Some sources say they were formally married, others dispute this.

Children: They had two children out of wedlock. Sarah was born in 1774. Their son died as an infant.

Interesting Highlights: The oldest Signer of the *Declaration of Independence* at 70, and of the *Constitution* at 83.

Developed first street lights in Philadelphia.

Founder of the University of Pennsylvania.

Organized first postal system in America and was Deputy Postmaster General in the Colonies from 1737 to 1752.

Organized the first volunteer fire department in America.

Was the fifteenth of seventeen children in his family.

Made a motion that Congress be opened each day with a prayer.

Last official act was his recommendation to Congress that they should formally abolish slavery.

Quotable Quote: *"In the beginning of the Contest with Great Britain, when we were sensible of the danger we had daily prayer ... for the Divine protection. Our prayers ... were heard, and they were graciously answered."*

Heroic Deed: Signing the *Declaration*. Benjamin Franklin knew that should the struggle for independence fail, an ignominious death by hanging would most certainly be his punishment.

Refused offer of amnesty from British Governor Gage in June 1775.

Little Known Fact: Sickly and frail when he signed the *Constitution*, he had to be carried in chair from his home to sessions of the Constitutional

Convention. Prisoners incarcerated in the city jail were recruited to undertake this task.

Price Paid for Signing: All the Signers, including Franklin, suffered monetary losses because of their connection with the cause. Some were brought to the brink of financial ruin, or even worse, abject poverty.

Thomas Jefferson
(1743 – 1826)

Heritage: Born in Virginia. Family was among the early immigrants to the Colonies. Ancestors were from Wales. Mother was of Scottish descent.

Religion: Christian (See quote below).

Education: Privately tutored in the classics as a young man. Attended William and Mary College. Graduated after only two years. Tutored in law by eminent attorney, George Wythe, who was a fellow Signer of the *Declaration*.

Marriage: Married independently wealthy widow, Martha Skelton on January 1, 1772. She was the 23-year old daughter of an eminent Virginia lawyer.

Children: Martha had one child that died as an infant during her first marriage. She and Thomas had five more, the last born in November of 1779.

Interesting Highlights: One of 49 men to sign the *Declaration of Independence* on August 2, 1776. Hancock was *only* man to sign on July 4. Six others signed at a later date – they were Gerry, Richard Henry Lee, McKean, Thornton, Wolcott and Wythe.

An accomplished scholar, he read several languages with ease.

Founded the University of Virginia and actually designed the buildings.

Died exactly 50 years after the adoption of the *Declaration of Independence* on July 4, 1826, as did fellow signer, John Adams.

Those who knew him best said he *never ever* lost his temper.

First man to propose laws in the Virginia legislature prohibiting the importation of slaves.

Lacked the charisma enjoyed by so many of the other political leaders.

Quotable Quote: *"I am a Christian in the only sense in which He wished anyone to be, sincerely attached to His doctrine in preference to all others."*

Heroic Deed: Signing the *Declaration of Independence*. Thomas Jefferson knew that should the struggle for independence fail, an ignominious death by hanging would most certainly be his punishment.

Refused an offer of amnesty from British Governor Gage in June 1775

Little Known Facts: Skillful performer on a violin.

Last words: *"I resign myself to my God, and my child to my country."*

First President to serve meringue pies for White House State dinners.

Price Paid for Signing: All the Signers, including Jefferson, suffered monetary losses because of their connection with the cause. Some were brought to the brink of financial ruin, or even worse, abject poverty. Sadly enough, Jefferson was so desperately in need of money before he died that he had to sell his magnificent library to the government for a mere $30,000.

Samuel Adams
(1722 – 1803)

Heritage: English. Born in Boston. Pilgrim ancestors. Descendant of Henry Adams who fled from religious persecution during the reign of

Charles 1. Related to John Alden who sailed to America on the Mayflower.

Religion: Christian. He once said: *"The rights of the Colonists as Christians ... may be best*

understood by reading and carefully studying ... the New Testament." Also see quote below.

Education: Tutored at the prestigious Boston Latin School. Entered Harvard when 14 and graduated with honors in 1740 when only 18.

Marriage: Twice married. In October of 1749, he married 24-year old Elizabeth Checkley. She died on July 25, 1757. On December 6, 1757, he remarried, this time to 29-year old Elizabeth Wells.

Children: He and his first wife had five children. Only two, Hannah and Samuel, Jr., lived to maturity.

Interesting Highlights: He and his cousin, John Adams, were two of the 49 men who signed the *Declaration of Independence* on August 2, 1776. Six others signed the *Declaration* at a later date. They were Gerry, Richard Henry Lee, McKean, Thornton, Wolcott and Wythe. John Hancock was only man to sign on July 4.

He once said: *"The right to freedom is a gift of the Almighty."*

Offered the resolution for a First Continental Congress that was convened in Carpenter's Hall, Philadelphia, on September 5, 1774.

Best known as *"The Father of the American Revolution."*

Quotable Quote: After signing the *Declaration*: *"We have this day restored the Sovereign to whom all men ought to be obedient."*

Heroic Deed: Signing the *Declaration*. Samuel Adams knew that should the struggle for independence fail, an ignominious death by hanging would most certainly be his punishment.

Refused offer of amnesty from British Governor Gage in June 1775.

Little Known Fact: Samuel Adams made this statement: *"The Constitution shall never be construed ... to prevent the people of the United States who are peaceable citizens from keeping their own arms."*

Price Paid for Signing: He and John Hancock were the only men not offered amnesty in 1775 by British Governor Gage. They were to be captured and severely punished because their *"offenses were of too flagitious a Nature to admit of any other Consideration than that of condign Punishment.*

Robert Morris
(1733 – 1806)

Heritage: English. His father, a Liverpool merchant, immigrated to America sometime in the mid-1700s. A very young Robert was left behind in the care of his grandmother. He was sent for at the age of 13-years.

Religion: Christian. His wife was the daughter of the late venerable Bishop of Pennsylvania.

Education: Placed in private school in Philadelphia. Chided by father for his slowness in learning, Robert replied: *"Why, sir, I have learned all that he could teach me."* The 15-year old was placed in the exporting business. With no more formal education, he became one of the richest men in the Colonies.

Marriage: Wed to Mary White in 1769. He was 35, she 20. Mary was from a wealthy, socially prominent Philadelphia family. She was described as *"tall, graceful and commanding, with a stately dignity of manner."*

Children: Five sons and two daughters. Some sources disagree and say they had only four children – three sons and one daughter.

Interesting Highlights: One of 56 men to sign the *Declaration of Independence*. Hancock was the *only* one to sign on July 4, 1776. Another 49 signed on August 2. Six signed at a later date – they were Richard Henry Lee, Gerry, McKean, Thorton, Wolcott and Wythe.

One of six men to sign both the *Declaration of Independence* and the *Constitution*. The others were Clymer, Franklin, Read, Sherman and Wilson.

One of six to sign both the *Constitution* and *Articles of Confederation*. The others were Daniel Carroll, Dickinson, Gouverneur Morris and Sherman.

One of only two men to sign all three of our nation's basic documents – the *Declaration of Independence, Constitution* and *Articles of Confederation*. The other Signer was Robert Sherman.

Quotable Quote: Astonished and indignant upon hearing about the Battle of Lexington, he said this: *"I vow to dedicate the rest of my life to the cause of freedom."*

Heroic Deed: Signing the *Declaration*. Robert Morris knew that should the struggle for

independence fail, an ignominious death by hanging would most certainly be his punishment.

Refused an offer of amnesty from British Governor Gage in June 1775.

Little Known Fact: One of two Signers of the *Declaration of Independence* who was born in England. The other was Button Gwinnett.

Price Paid for Signing: All the Signers, including Robert Morris, suffered monetary losses because of their connection with the cause. Some were brought to the brink of financial ruin, or even worse, abject poverty.

Benjamin Rush
(1745 – 1813)

Heritage: English. Born at Berberry, about 12 miles northeast of Philadelphia. His father, an officer in Cromwell's army, immigrated to America from England during the late 1600s or early 1700s.

Religion: Christian. He explained it in this manner: *"I have alternately been called an Aristocrat and a Democrat. I am neither, I am a Christocrat."* Cofounder of the **Philadelphia Bible Society**, a group that strongly advocated using the *Bible* and *Scripture* in all public schools. Also see quote below.

Education: Attended prestigious West Nottingham Academy in Rising Sun, Maryland. Graduated with honors from the College of New Jersey (now Princeton) in 1760 when just 15-years old. Then returned to Philadelphia and began an apprenticeship with a prominent physician.

Marriage: Married Julie Stockton on January 11, 1776. Oldest daughter of another zealous patriot, Richard Stockton, also. a Signer of the *Declaration.*

Children: They had 13 children, all of whom survived him. Some sources say only six sons and three daughters survived him.

Interesting Highlights: One of 56 men to sign the *Declaration of Independence.* Hancock was the *only* one to sign on July 4, 1776. Another 49 signed on August 2. Six signed at a later date – they were Richard Henry Lee, Gerry, McKean, Thorton, Wolcott and Wythe.

One of *the* youngest Signers of the *Declaration* at 30 years of age.

Served his country as Surgeon General in the Continental Army. Resigned after a disagreement with General Washington.

Helped found the *Pennsylvania Society for Promoting the Abolition of Slavery* in 1787. Later served as the organization's President.

Quotable Quote: His last words before dying: *"... blessed Jesus, wash away all my impurities, and receive me into Thy everlasting kingdom."*

Heroic Deed: Signing the *Declaration*. Benjamin Rush knew that should the struggle for independence fail, an ignominious death by hanging would most certainly be his punishment.

Refused an offer of amnesty from British Governor Gage in June 1775.

Little Known Fact: In 1776, he suggested to Thomas Paine that he should write his famous book, **COMMON SENSE**. He even gave Paine the title and helped finance its publication.

Died during a typhus epidemic in 1813 at the age of 67.

Price Paid for Signing: All the Signers, including Rush, suffered monetary losses because of their connection with the cause. Some were brought to the brink of financial ruin, or even worse, abject poverty.

Richard Henry Lee
(1732 – 1794)

Heritage: English. Direct descendant of early settlers un the Virginia Colony who had emigrated from England to America in the early 1600s.

Religion: A man of strong Christian convictions. Was known as a sincere practicing Christian. His character was above reproach.

Education: Father sent him to England as a young boy to get his education. Had the finest tutors and attended the most prestigious private schools. Returned to Virginia a polished scholar when nearly 19-years of age.

Marriage: Twice married. First married Anne Aylett in 1757. Her father was a close friend and advisor to General George Washington. Her mother and Martha Washington were first cousins. She died in 1767 at the age of 35 years. He remarried in 1769, this time to Anne Pincard.

Children: Had 4 children – 2 boys and 2 girls in his first marriage. His second wife bore him 5 more children – 3 girls and 2 more sons.

Interesting Highlights: First man in Virginia to publicly denounce the British Stamp Act.

One of 56 men to sign the *Declaration of Independence*. Hancock was the *only* one to sign on July 4, 1776. Another 49 signed on August 2. Six signed at a later date – they were Lee, Gerry, McKean, Thorton, Wolcott and Wythe.

His younger brother, Francis Lightfoot, was also a signer of the *Declaration.*

He and fellow patriot, Patrick Henry, were the closest of friends

Lee and Henry, young America's greatest orator, opposed ratifying the *Constitution* unless specific Amendments were added.

Ludwell, one of Lee's sons, was on the staff of General Lafayette.

Lee became Virginia's first Senator under the new *Constitution.*

Quotable Quote: Regarding guns, he said: *"To preserve liberty, it is essential that the whole body of the people always possess arms, and be taught alike, especially when young, how to use them."*

Heroic Deed: Signing the *Declaration.* Richard Henry Lee knew that should the struggle for independence fail, an ignominious death by hanging would most certainly be his punishment.

Refused offer of amnesty from British Governor Gage in June 1775.

Little Known Fact: He was the daring Colonial patriot who bravely introduced the first *Resolution for Independence* before the Continental

Congress in July 2, 1776. John Adams immediately seconded it.

Price Paid for Signing: All the Signers, including Lee, suffered monetary losses because of their connection with the cause. Some were brought to the brink of financial ruin, or even worse, abject poverty.

Samuel Chase
(1722 – 1811)

Heritage: English. Born in Somerset County, Maryland. Family immigrated to America from England in the late 1600s or early 1700s.

Religion: Devout Christian. Son of an Anglican clergyman, a minister of the Protestant Episcopal Church. Also see quote below.

Education: Avid reader of everything he could get his hands on as a child and young adult. Father provided him with a basic education in the classics. Studied at home with the best of private tutors. Studied law under the auspices of Messrs. Hammond and Hall, the most prestigious law firm in the Annapolis area.

Marriage: Twice married. Wed first to Anne Baldwin in 1762. She died right after the Revolutionary War started. Second marriage was to Hannah Kilty Giles in 1783. She was a lovely young woman he met while on a business trip to London.

Children: Samuel and Anne had six children – two sons and four daughters. Second wife, Hannah, bore him two daughters.

Interesting Highlights: Voted for acceptance of the *Declaration of Independence* on July 2, 1776.

One of 56 men to sign the *Declaration of Independence.* Hancock was the *only* one to sign on July 4, 1776. Another 49 signed on August 2. Six signed at a later date – they were Richard Henry Lee, Gerry, McKean, Thorton, Wolcott and Wythe.

Had law practice with William Paca, later also to be a delegate to the Continental Congress and fellow Signer of the *Declaration of Independence.*

Chairman of special congressional committee formed to punish Americans who were known to have given "aid and comfort to the enemy."

Quotable Quote: An 1848 textbook described him this way: *"Judge Chase was a* *man of great benevolence of feeling and in all his walks, he exemplified the beauties of Christianity, of which he was a sincere professor."*

Heroic Deed: Signing the *Declaration*. Samuel Chase knew that should the struggle for independence fail, an ignominious death by hanging would most certainly be his punishment.

Refused an offer of amnesty from British Governor Gage in June 1775.

Little Known Fact: Samuel Chase said this: *"By our form of government, the Christian religion is the established religion; and all sects and denominations of Christians are placed upon the same equal footing, and are equally entitled to protection in their religious liberty."*

Price Paid for Signing: All the Signers, including Chase, suffered monetary losses because of their connection with the cause. Some were brought to the brink of financial ruin, or even worse, abject poverty.

John Witherspoon
(1722 or 1723 – 1794)

Heritage: Scottish. Born in a small village near Edinburgh. Descendant of the Great Reformer, John Knox. Immigrated to America in 1768.

Religion: Christian. Son of a Calvinist clergyman who was pastor of a Scottish Church of Yester. Licensed preacher.

Education: Tutored in exclusive private school in Haddington. Theological studies at

 University of Edinburgh when 14 years old. Masters degree in 1739. Divinity degree at age 20 in 1743.

Marriage: Twice married. First wife in 1783. She died in 1789. Wed again at 68 years in 1791 to a 24-year old widow.

Children: 10 children born in first marriage. Five died before the family immigrated to America. Had two more children with second wife.

Interesting Highlights: Signed the *Declaration of Independence* on August 2, 1776. Hancock was *only* man to sign on July 4.

One of the four Signers who had been trained for the ministry. The others were Hall, Hooper and Paine.

Held distinction of being the *only* active clergyman among the Signers.

One of the eight foreign born Signers. The others were Gwinnett, Lewis, Robert Morris, Smith, Taylor, Thornton and Wilson.

One of only two of the Signers to have been born in Scotland. The other was the distinguished James Wilson.

Served on more than 100 committees in the Continental Congress.

President of the College of New Jersey (presently Princeton).

Quotable Quote: John Adams called him *"A true son of liberty. So he was. But first, he was a Son of the Cross."*

Heroic Deed: Signing the *Declaration*. John Witherspoon knew that should the struggle for independence fail, an ignominious death by hanging would most certainly be his punishment.

Refused offer of amnesty from British Governor Gage in June 1775.

Little Known Fact: Oldest son, James, served in Continental Army as an aide to General Nash. Killed during the Battle of Germantown.

Second son, John, went down with a ship at sea in 1795.

Lost eyesight two years prior to his death. Had to be assisted to the pulpit. Still able to preach a sermon with all the vigor of his youthful years.

Punishment: When the British occupied New Jersey in November of 1776, they used Princeton to billet their troops and stable their horses.

Everything was wantonly destroyed and all library books were burned.

Elbridge Gerry
(1744 -- 1814)

Heritage: English descent. Born in Marblehead, Massachusetts, on July 17, the third of 12 children.

Religion: Devout Christian. Attended church regularly. Brought up in a home where the *Bible* was read nightly.

Education: Father resolved to making certain his son got the best possible education. Attended only the finest of prep schools. Attended Harvard and graduated in 1762 when just 18-years old.

Marriage: Wed a beautiful Irish girl, Ann Thompson, of New York while a member of the Continental Congress. Graduate of University of Edinburg in Scotland. She was a high society favorite.

Children: Nine children – six daughters and three sons.

Interesting Highlights: One of 56 men to sign the *Declaration of Independence*. Hancock was the *only* one to sign on July 4, 1776. Another 49

153

signed on August 2. Six signed at a later date – they were Gerry, Richard Henry Lee, McKean, Thorton, Wolcott and Wythe.

Not a shy man, he spoke a total of 119 times while a delegate to the Continental Congress.

A most vocal members of the 1787 Constitutional Convention. Said one delegate: *"He objected to everything he did not propose."*

Quotable Quote: At the adoption of the *Declaration of Independence* on July 4, 1776, Hancock declared: *"We must all hang together [stick] together."* Franklin smilingly responded with: *"Yes, we must all hang together, or most assuredly, we shall hang separately."* It was at this point that the very large Benjamin Harrison with a tinkle in his eyes looked over at smallish Elbridge Gerry and said: *"With me it will be over in a minute, but you, you will be dancing on air an hour after I am gone.."*

Heroic Deed: Signing the *Declaration*. Elbridge Gerry knew that should the struggle for independence fail, an ignominious death by hanging would most certainly be his punishment.

Refused offer of amnesty from British Governor Gage in June 1775.

Little Known Fact: His wife, Ann, was the last surviving wife of a Signer of the *Declaration of Independence.*

Price Paid for Signing: All the Signers, including Gerry, suffered monetary losses because of their connection with the cause. Some were brought to the brink of financial ruin, or even worse, abject poverty.

Francis Lewis
(1713 – 1803)

Heritage: Welsh. Born in Llandaff, Glamoganshire, Wales. Orphaned when about 5-years old. Brought up by maiden aunt. Immigrated to America from Wales sometime around 1734 when he was 21-years old.

Religion: Devout Christian. Only child of an Episcopal minister. Mother was a minister's daughter. See quote below.

Education: Portion of his education was obtained in Scotland while living there with a relative. Became proficient in his native tongue (the ancient Briton) as well as in the Gaelic language, then mostly used in Scotland. His uncle, Dean of St. Paul's in London, eventually sent him to prestigious Westminister to obtain a well-rounded education.

Marriage: Wed Elizabeth Annesely in 1745, a New York girl who was the sister of his business partner.

Children: Three. – two sons, Frances and Morgan; one daughter, Ann. Some sources say they actually had seven children.

Interesting Highlights: One of 56 men to sign the *Declaration of Independence.* Hancock was the *only* one to sign on July 4, 1776. Another 49 signed on August 2. Six signed at a later date – they were Richard Henry Lee, Gerry, McKean, Thorton, Wolcott and Wythe.

Only Signer of the *Declaration* to have been born in Wales.

Inherited money when 21 and invested in a great deal of merchandise. Only 21 at this time, he sailed with his merchandise to America. A highly successful business partnership was then set up in New York.

Quotable Quote: *"I agree, without reservation, with my colleague, Hamilton, who said: 'I have carefully examined the evidences of the Christian religion, and if I was sitting as a juror upon its authenticity I would unhesitatingly give my verdict in its favor.' "*

Heroic Deed: Signing the *Declaration.* Francis Lewis knew that should the struggle for independence fail, an ignominious death by hanging would most certainly be his punishment.

Refused offer of amnesty from British Governor Gage in June 1775.

Little Known Fact: Unselfishly used much of his fortune to support the American Revolution.

Seldom spoke during the debates in the Continental Congress.

Price Paid for Signing: British thugs were sent out "to seize the lady and devastate the property." They burned everything found in the house and kidnapped his wife, Elizabeth. She was beaten often and severely. Her early death is attributed to the inhuman treatment she received from her British captors.

Roger Sherman
(1721 – 1793)

Heritage: English descent. Born in Newton, Massachusetts. Parents immigrated to the Colonies from England in the late 1600s or early 1700s.

Religion: John Adams described Sherman as *"...an old Puritan, as honest as an angel ...."* **Education**: Early formal education extremely limited. Avid reader. Self-taught in mathematics, astronomy and numerous other subjects.

Always kept books open on the workbench while repairing shoes. Studied law by reading books borrowed from local attorneys.

Marriage: Twice married. Wed first wife, Elizabeth Hartwell, in 1749. He was 28. Little is known about She died 11 years later in 1760. Remarried, this time to Rebecca Prescott. She was 20 and he was 42.

Children: Seven children born to first union. Eight more born to he and second wife. All but one lived to maturity.

Interesting Highlights: One of 56 men to sign the *Declaration of Independence*. Hancock was the *only* one to sign on July 4, 1776. Another 49 signed on August 2. Six signed at a later date – they were Richard Henry Lee, Gerry, McKean, Thorton, Wolcott and Wythe.
One of six Signers who also affixed his signature to the *Constitution*. The others were Clymer, Franklin, Robert Morris, Read and Wilson.

Seconded Benjamin Franklin's motion that Congress be opened each day with a prayer.

Made an astounding 128 speeches at the Constitutional Convention.

Quotable Quote: *"I believe there is one only living and true God, existing in three persons, the Father, the Son, and the Holy Ghost ... that the Scriptures of the old and new testaments are a* *revelation from God, and a complete rule to direct us as how we may glorify and enjoy him."*

`**Heroic Deed:** Signing the *Declaration*. Roger Sherman knew that should the struggle for independence fail, an ignominious death by hanging would most certainly be his punishment.

Refused offer of amnesty from British Governor Gage in June 1775

Little Known Fact: Only man to sign all four founding documents: *Articles of Association* (1774); *Declaration of Independence* (1776); *Articles of Confederation* (1777) and *Constitution* (1787).

Price Paid for Signing: All the Signers, including Sherman, suffered monetary losses because of their connection with the cause. Some were brought to the brink of financial ruin, or even worse, abject poverty.

George Taylor (1716 – 1781)

Heritage: Irish. Born in Ireland. Immigrated to America from Ireland in 1773. Settled in Pennsylvania.

Religion: Devout Christian. Son of a clergyman. It isn't known if he was Protestant or Roman Catholic. See quote below.

Education: Primarily self-taught through extensive reading. Some home schooling by various tutors. An extremely bright young man, he taught himself fluent Latin as well as numerous subjects on running a business.

Marriage: Married a widow, Nancy Savage, in 1742. Nancy died in 1768. George never remarried. Had long-standing affair with housekeeper. Why they didn't marry is unknown.

Children: He and Nancy had three children – two sons and a daughter. Taylor and his housekeeper had five children out of wedlock.

Interesting Highlights: One of 56 men to sign the *Declaration of Independence*. Hancock was the *only* one to sign on July 4, 1776. Another 49 signed on August 2. Six signed at a later date – they were Richard Henry Lee, Gerry, McKean, Thorton, Wolcott and Wythe.

One three signers of the *Declaration of Independence* to be born in Ireland. The other two were Smith and Thornton.

One of eight signers of the *Declaration* who were foreign born. The others were: Gwinnett, Lewis, Robert Morris, Smith, Thornton, Wilson and Witherspoon.

In 1776, his Durham Iron Works made cannons and cannon balls for the Continental Army.

Elected to the Colonial Assembly in 1764 and was a member when the British imposed the notorious *Stamp Act* in March of 1765.

Quotable Quote: *"I do not believe the Bible can have a value placed upon it. God's Holy Book is worth more to me than all other books that have ever been published throughout the world."*

Heroic Deed: Signing the *Declaration of Independence*. George Taylor knew that should the struggle for independence fail, an ignominious death by hanging would most certainly be his punishment.

Refused offer of amnesty from British Governor Gage in June 1775.

Little Known Fact: Only *Signer* to have run away from home and came to America as a *"redemptioner,"* more commonly known as an indentured servant.

Price Paid for Signing: All the Signers, including Taylor, suffered monetary losses because of their connection with the cause. Some were brought to the brink of financial ruin, or even worse, abject poverty.

Caesar Rodney
(1728 – 1784)

Heritage: English. Born in Dover, Delaware, son of wealthy plantation owner. Grandfather emigrated from England to America soon after William Penn started settlement of Pennsylvania.

Religion: Christian. See quote below.

Education: A brilliant, self-educated man. Tutored at home. Inherited his father's plantation in 1745 when just 17-years old. Had to devote his time to running business affairs.

Marriage: Never married.

Interesting Highlights: Opposed the tyrannical Stamp Act of 1765.

One of 56 men to sign the *Declaration of Independence.* Hancock was the *only* one to sign on July 4, 1776. Another 49 signed on August 2. Six signed at a later date – they were Richard Henry Lee, Gerry, McKean, Thorton, Wolcott and Wythe.

Described by a fellow Signer of the *Declaration of Independence* as *"an animated skeleton with a bandaged head."*

One of two bachelors to sign the *Declaration of Independence.* The other was Joseph Hewes of North Carolina.

Became Major General in the Continental Army in September, 1777.

Delegate to the Second Continental Congress that convened in the Philadelphia State House on May 10, 1775.

Quotable Quote: Instrumental in having this Article included in the *Constitution* of Delaware: *"Every person who shall be chosen a member of either house, or appointed to any office or place of trust ... shall ... make and subscribe the following declaration, to wit: 'I, _____, do profess faith in God the Father, and in Jesus Christ His only Son, and in the Holy Ghost, one God, blessed for evermore; I do acknowledge the holy scriptures of the Old and New Testament to be given by divine inspiration'."*

Heroic Deed: Signing the *Declaration of Independence*. Caesar Rodney knew that should the struggle for independence fail, an ignominious death by hanging would most certainly be his punishment.

Refused an offer of amnesty from British Governor Gage in June 1775.

Little Known Fact: Suffered since childhood with disfiguring, painful, unsightly cancer that was eating away his face. Covered this with a green silk scarf when in public. This is the reason he never tried to marry.

Price Paid for Signing: All the Signers, including Rodney, suffered monetary losses because of their connection with the cause. Some were brought to the brink of financial ruin, or even worse, abject poverty

Philip Livingston (1716 – 1778)

Heritage: Scottish-Dutch. Born in Albany, New York, to one of the wealthiest and most politically powerful families in the Colonies. Descendants immigrated to America from Rotterdam, Holland, sometime in the late 1600s.

Religion: Christian. Descendant of a Scottish minister.

Education: Tutored by his maternal grandmother. Attended Yale. Graduated with distinguished honors in 1737 when 21-years old.

Marriage: Wed to Christina Ten Broech about 1740. She was a woman of sturdy Dutch stock.

Children: Had nine children.

Interesting Highlights: Initially opposed independence.

Delegate to the First Continental Congress that convened on September 5, 1774, in Carpenter's Hall, Philadelphia.

One of 56 men to sign the *Declaration of Independence*. Hancock was the *only* one to sign on July 4, 1776. Another 49 signed on August 2. Six signed at a later date – they were Richard Henry Lee, Gerry, McKean, Thorton, Wolcott and Wythe.

One son, Henry, served as an aide to General Washington.

Abraham, their eighth child, served in the Continental Army. He was captured by the British and incarcerated in Charleston, South Carolina.

After State governments were formed, he was elected a member of New York's first Senate that met on September 10, 1777..

Quotable Quote: John Adams wrote of this man in his diary: *"Philip Livingston is a great, rough, rapid mortal. There is no holding any conversation with him. He blusters away – says if England should turn us adrift, we should instantly go to civil war among ourselves, to determine which Colony should govern all the rest."*
Heroic Deed: Signing the *Declaration*. Philip Livingston knew that should the struggle for independence fail, an ignominious death by hanging would most certainly be his punishment.

Refused offer of amnesty from British Governor Gage in June 1775.

Little Known Fact: His younger brother, William, signed the United States *Constitution*.

Price Paid for Signing: Lost most of his business property, two homes and his family as a result of his unselfish devotion to his dream of a new America free of British tyranny. He died a heart-broken man at the age of 62, still separated from his family by the Revolutionary War.

Francis Hopkinson
(1737 – 1791)

Heritage: English. Born in Philadelphia. Family immigrated to America from England sometime in the late 1600s or early 1700s.

Religion: Devout Christian. Mother was daughter of England's Bishop of Worcester. Also see quote below.

Education: Tutored by his mother until ready to attend the College of Philadelphia (now the University of Pennsylvania). After graduation in 1757, was tutored in law by prominent attorney Benjamin Chew.

Marriage: Wed wealthy Ann Borden of Bordenton, New Jersey, on September 5, 1768. Father operated a stage coach line and boat business.

Children: Nine. Three died as infants.

Interesting Highlights: Delegate to the Second Continental Congress that convened on May 10, 1775 at the State House in Philadelphia.

One of 56 men to sign the *Declaration of Independence*. Hancock was the *only* one to sign on July 4, 1776. Another 49 signed on August 2. Six signed at a later date – they were Richard Henry Lee, Gerry, McKean, Thorton, Wolcott and Wythe.

Credited with designing the Stars and Stripes in 1777.

Became the most widely known poet, musician, artist, satirical essayist and writer in the Colonies.

Drew caricatures of his colleagues during sessions of the Continental Congress in an effort to relieve his boredom and stay alert.

Wife a fervent patriot and leader of the *New York Revolutionary Convention.*

Wife's sister, Maria, married Thomas McKean, a fellow Signer of the *Declaration of Independence.*

Quotable Quote: *"This land, America, was our Father's gift from heaven. It has been decreed to us by Divine Providence. There can be no other explanation."*

Heroic Deeds: Signing the *Declaration*. Francis Hopkinson knew that should the struggle for independence fail, an ignominious death by hanging would most certainly be his punishment.

Refused offer of amnesty from British Governor Gage in June 1775.

Little Known Fact: Wrote a book titled ***The Prophecy.*** In it he predicted the adoption of the *Declaration of Independence.*

Price Paid for Signing: All the Signers, including Hopkinson, suffered monetary losses because of their connection with the cause. Some were brought to the brink of financial ruin, or even worse, abject poverty.

Francis Lightfoot Lee (1734 – 1797)

Heritage: English.   Born in Virginia. Direct descendant of early settlers in the Virginia Colony who had immigrated to America from England sometime in the early 1600s.

Religion: Known as a man of extremely strong Christian conviction.

Education: Solely educated by a private tutor – an eminent Scottish clergyman, the Reverend Doctor Clapp. His father died before he

was old enough to be sent abroad to study as was his brother, Richard Henry.

Marriage: Wed 19-year old socialite, Rebecca Taylor, in 1769.

Children: They had no children.

Interesting Highlights: Delegate to Continental Congress.

One of 56 men to sign the *Declaration of Independence*. Hancock was *only* one to sign on July 4, 1776. Another 49 signed on August 2. Six signed at later date – they were Richard Henry Lee, Gerry, McKean, Thorton, Wolcott and Wythe.

Younger brother of fellow Signer, Richard Henry Lee.

Vigorously opposed the institution of slavery in the Colonies.

Not a fluent speaker as was his polished brother, Richard Henry.

Rarely took part in debates on the floor of the Continental Congress because of his shyness.

Signed both the *Declaration of Independence* and the *Articles of Confederation*.

Quotable Quote: *"For one to sincerely believe in the Lord Jesus Christ, is to live happily and with little worry. This I do without reservation. I unquestionably enjoy the peace on mind He brings to me. I trust Him fully."*

Heroic Deed: Signing the *Declaration*. Francis Lightfoot Lee knew that should the struggle for Independence fail, an ignominious death by hanging would most be his punishment.

Refused offer of amnesty from British Governor Gage in June 1775.

Little Known Fact: Relied on the judgment of his older brother, Richard Henry Lee. Held him up as a role model.

Price Paid for Signing: All the Signers, including Lee, suffered monetary losses because of their connection with the cause. Some were brought to the brink of financial ruin, or even worse, abject poverty.

10

Enticing Tidbits

Of

Constitutional Trivia

A Few Exciting Tidbits
Of Constitutional Trivia

The Constitutional Convention met at Independence Hall *(the State House)* on May 14, 1787, to revise the *Articles of Confederation* and formulate the *Constitution*.

George Washington had been unanimously elected President of the Convention. He abruptly arose during the Convention and admonished the delegates: *"If to please the people, we offer what we ourselves disapprove, how can we afterward defend our work? Let us raise a standard to which the wise and the honest can repair; the event is in the Hand of God!"*

The Constitution has 4,400 words.

It is the oldest and shortest written *Constitution* of any government in the world.

The word *"democracy"* does not appear once in the *Constitution*.

When the *Constitution* was signed, the United States' population was 4 million.

It is now more than 300 million.

173

Philadelphia was the nation's largest city, with 40,000 inhabitants.

Gouverneur Morris was largely responsible for the "wording" of the *Constitution*, although there was a *Committee of Style* formed in September 1787.

The following events took place in the Pennsylvania State House in Philadelphia:

a.   The Constitutional Convention was held.

b.George Washington was appointed the Commander of the Continental Army in 1775.

The *Constitution* was "penned" by a man named Jacob Shallus.

a.   Shallus was a Pennsylvania Assembly clerk who transcribed the document for a $30.00 fee *(This amount would be equal to $280 today).*

b. It took 100 Days for Shallus to actually "frame" *(finish outlining) the Constitution.*

c. *"Pensylnvania"* (Pennsylvania) right above the various signatures is a glaring mistake in spelling.

Neither Thomas Jefferson nor John Adams attended the *Constitutional Convention* or signed the *Constitution.*

a. Jefferson was in France where he served as the U.S. minister.

b. Adams was in Great Britain where he served as the U.S. minister.

Patrick Henry was elected as a delegate to the *Constitutional Convention,* but declined, because he *"smelt a rat."*

James Madison, best known as *"the Father of the Constitution,"* was the first to arrive in Philadelphia for the *Constitutional Convention.*

a.   He arrived in February, three months before the *Constitutional Convention* actually began.

b. He developed blueprint for the new *Constitution.*

c. Was the only delegate to attend every meeting.

d.   Took detailed notes of the various discussions and debates that took place during the convention.

e. The journal that he kept during the *Constitutional Convention* was kept secret until after he died.

f.   It (along with other papers) was purchased by the government in 1837 at a price of $30,000 *(that would be $404,828.99 today).*

g. His journal was published in 1840.

h.   George Washington and James Madison were the only presidents who signed the *Constitution.*

Of the 42 delegates who attended most of the meetings, only 39 actually signed the *Constitution.*

The oldest man to sign the *Constitution* was Benjamin Franklin of Pennsylvania who was 81 at the time.

> a. Although Franklin's mind remained active, his body was deteriorating.
>
> b. He was in constant pain because of gout and having a stone in his bladder.
>
> c. He could barely walk

Franklin entered the Convention Hall in a sedan chair carried by four prisoners from the Walnut Street jail in Philadelphia.

> a. Because of his poor health, the elderly gentleman needed help to sign.
>
> b. As he affixed his signature, tears streamed down his face.

Franklin left the Pennsylvania State House after the final meeting of the Constitutional Convention on September 17, 1787.

a. He was approached by the wife of the mayor of Philadelphia. She was curious as to what the new government would be.

b. Franklin replied: *"A republic, madam. If you can keep it."*

Benjamin Franklin died on April 17, 1790, at the age of 84.

c. The 20,000 mourners at his funeral on April 21, 1790, constituted the largest public gathering up to that time.

When it came time for the States to ratify the *Constitution*, the lack of any *Bill of Rights* was the primary sticking point.

Ellbridge Gerry of Massachusetts refused to sign due in part to this fact.

The *Great Compromise,* authored by Connecticut delegate Roger Sherman, saved the *Constitutional Convention*, and, probably, the Union.

It called for proportional representation in the House, and one representative per state in the Senate *(this was later changed to two).*

The compromise passed 5-to-4, with one state, Massachusetts, *"divided."*

In November of 1788 the *Congress of the Confederation* adjourned.

a. The United States was left without a central government until April 1789.

b. This when the first Congress under the new *Constitution* convened with its first quorum.

c. It called for proportional representation in the House, and one representative per state in the Senate *(this was later changed to two)*.

d. The compromise passed 5-to-4, with one state, Massachusetts, *"divided."*

On March 24, 1788, a popular election was held in Rhode Island to determine the ratification status of the new *Constitution.* The vote was 237 in favor and 2,945 opposed!

Vermont, although not yet having become a State, ratified the *Constitution* on January 10,1791.

The youngest man to sign the *Constitution* was Jonathan Dayton of New Jersey who was only 26 at the time.

James Wilson originally proposed the President be chosen by popular vote.

a. The delegates disagreed.

b. After 60 ballots, they finally approved a system.

c. Thus was called the Electoral College.

Although there have been 500 proposed amendments to change it,

this *"indirect"* system of electing the president is still intact today.

There was initially a question as to how to address the President.

a. The Senate proposed that he be addressed as *"His Highness the President of the United States of America and Protector of their Liberties."*

b. Both the House of Representatives and the Senate compromised on the use of *"President of the United States."*

The members of the first Congress of the United States included:

a. 54 who were delegates to the *Constitutional Convention*

b. Or delegates to the various state-ratifying conventions.

c. The number also included 7 delegates who opposed ratification.

There was a proposal at the *Constitutional Convention* to limit the standing army for the country to 5,000 men. George Washington sarcastically agreed with this proposal as long as a stipulation was added that no invading army could number more than 3,000 troops!

Washington wrote to the Marquis de Lafayette that *"It* (the Constitution) *appears to me, then, little short of a miracle."*

 John Adams referred to the *Constitution* as *"the greatest single effort of national deliberation that the world has ever seen."*

A proclamation by President George Washington and a Congressional Resolution established the first national Thanksgiving Day on November 26, 1789. The reason for the holiday was to give *"thanks"* for the new *Constitution.*

The *Constitution* was stored in various cities until 1952, when it was placed in the National Archives Building in Washington, D.C.

a. The entire *Constitution* is displayed only one day a year—September 17, the anniversary of the day the framers signed the document.

b. During the daytime, pages one and four of the document are displayed in a bullet-proof case.

c. Case contains helium and water vapor to preserve the paper's quality.

d. At night, the pages are lowered into a vault, behind five-ton doors that are designed to withstand a nuclear explosion.

During an event to celebrate the Constitution's Sesquicentennial in 1937, Harry F. Wilhelm recited the entire document through the newly added 21st Amendment from memory.   He then obtained a job in the Sesquicentennial mailroom!

11

An Outline Sketch

Of

Each Signer

Of

Our Constitution

Abraham Baldwin
(1754 – 1807)

Heritage: English and Scots. Born at Guilford, Connecticut. Family immigrated to America sometime in the late 1600s or early 1700s.

Religion: Devout Christian. Chaplain in the Continental Army during the Revolutionary War. Became a tutor and minister at Yale (1775 -- 1779).

Education: Getting his son a proper education was of the utmost importance to his blacksmith father, who went heavily in debt to pay for this.

Attended nearby village school. Also taught by the best private tutors. A brilliant scholar, he graduated with honors from Yale in 1772. Later studied law.

Marriage: None. Was a bachelor.

Children: None.

Interesting Highlights: Coming from a rather humble background, he was highly successful as a clergyman, lawyer, teacher and politician.

One of 39 men who signed the *Constitution*.

One of three Signers of the *Constitution* who was a lifelong bachelor. The others were Gilman and Jenifer. Two bachelors signed the *Declaration of Independence.* They were Hewes and Rodney.

Turned down the offer to be the Professor of Divinity at Yale in 1781.

Founded Franklin College in 1798, a school that would later become the University of Georgia. Served as its first President.

Baldwin's half-brother, Henry, became a Justice on the United States Supreme Court.

Heroic Deed: In June of 1775, British Governor Gage made a desperate attempt to stem the tide of the blossoming independence movement. Amnesty was offered to every Colonist – with the exception of Samuel Adams and John Hancock – who would lay down their arms and swear loyalty to the Crown. To their credit, not one patriot, including Baldwin, turn coated and accepted the pardon.

Little Known Fact: Went on to serve for 18 years in the House of Representatives (1789 to 1799) and the Senate (1799 to 1807). Bitterly fought against the policies of Alexander Hamilton and was an ally of Jefferson and Madison.

Price Paid for Signing: All the Signers, including Baldwin, suffered monetary losses because of their connection with the cause. Some were brought to the brink of financial ruin, or even worse, abject poverty

Richard Bassett
(1745 – 1815)

Heritage: English. Born in Cecil County, Maryland. Family immigrated to America from England in the late 1600s or early 1700s.

Religion: Devout Christian. Became a Methodist while serving as a Captain in the Continental Army. Held many church services in his home, Bohemian Manor. Always supported his church financially. See quote below.

Education: Wealthy foster father made certain he received a decent education. Had only the best tutors while being home schooled during his youth. No record of attending college. Studied law in Philadelphia

Marriage: Twice wed. First wife was Ann Ennals, his second a woman named Bruff. Little is known about either of these women.

Children: Fathered an unknown number of children.

Interesting Highlights: Delegate to the *Constitutional Convention.*

Served on no committees and made no speeches during the debates in the Constitutional Convention.

Of the One of 39 men who signed the *Constitution*.

Raised by relative, Peter Lawson, after father abandoned the family.

Led the battle to get his State to ratify the *United States Constitution*. Efforts paid off on December 7, 1787. Delaware became the first to do so.

Raised a 10,000-man militia unit. This was to provide General Washington with assistance should it be needed to hold New York City

Captain in the cavalry militia of Dover, Delaware.

Heroic Deed: Refused an offer of amnesty from British Governor Gage in June 1775.

Little Known Fact: One of 12 Signers of the *Constitution* who owned slaves. The others were Blair, Blount, Butler, Carroll, Jenifer, Madison, Charles and Charles Cotesworth Pinckney, Rutledge, Spaight and Washington.

Advocated unrestricted slave trade while attending the Constitutional Convention held in Philadelphia from May 25 to September 17, 1787.

Price Paid for Signing: All the Signers, including Bassett,. suffered monetary losses because of their connection with the cause. Some were brought to the brink of financial ruin, or even worse, abject poverty.

Gunning Bedford
(1747 – 1812)

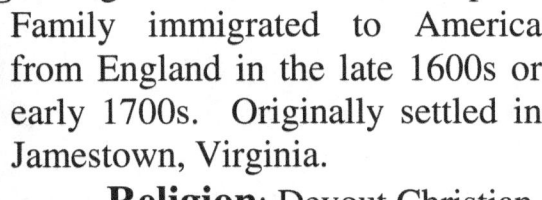

Heritage: English. Born in Philadelphia. Family immigrated to America from England in the late 1600s or early 1700s. Originally settled in Jamestown, Virginia.

Religion: Devout Christian.

Education: Had only the best private tutors as a child and young adult. Graduated with honors from the College of New Jersey (presently Princeton). Studied law under Joseph Read, a prominent Philadelphia attorney.

Marriage: Wed Jane B. Parker while attending Princeton.

Children: At least one child – a daughter.

Interesting Highlights: Delegate to the Constitutional Convention that convened in Philadelphia from May 25 to September 17, 1787

One of the best speakers and debaters at the Convention.

One of the most active members of the Constitutional Convention. Seldom missed a session of the Convention.

One of 39 men who signed the *Constitution*.

Close friend of fellow Signer of the *Constitution*, James Madison.

Madison was Bedford's roommate while attending the College of New Jersey (presently Princeton).

Bore arms during the War for Independence. Served in Continental Army as an aide to General Washington.

Delegate to the Continental Congress from 1783 to 1785.

Delegate to Annapolis Convention in 1785, but failed to attend and sessions. Was busy with other responsibilities.

Attended the Delaware Constitutional Convention where the *United States Constitution* was ratified.

President Washington appointed him to be a Federal District Judge for Maryland. Held this position until he died.

Heroic Deed: Refused offer of amnesty from British Governor Gage in June 1775.

Little Known Fact: One of numerous Founding Fathers who studied under John Witherspoon, Signer of the *Declaration of*

Independence, and leading scholar and theologian of the period.

Price Paid for Signing: All the Signers, including Bedford, suffered monetary losses because of their connection with the cause. Some were brought to the brink of financial ruin, or even worse, abject poverty.

John Blair
(1732 – 1800)

Heritage: Born in Williamsburg, Virginia. Descendants sailed to America from England and arrived sometime in the early 1600s.

Religion: Devout Christian. Episcopal. Very active in church. Supported his church generously.

Education: Attended only the finest private schools. Also tutored extensively. Graduated from William and Mary College. Went on to study law at the prestigious London's Middle Temple.

Marriage: A widower. His wife, Jean Balfour, died in 1792. He chose to honor the memory of his loving mate by not remarrying.

Children: None.

Interesting Highlights: One of 39 men who signed the *Constitution*.

Practiced law in Williamsburg, Virginia,

Father was a Colonial official.

Involved in the patriot movement for independence as early as 1770.

Uncle was founder and first president of College of William and Mary.

Delegate to the Constitutional Convention in 1787.

Religiously attended every session of the Convention, but took part in none of the committees.

Never made a speech at the Constitutional Convention due to his inherent shyness. He was somewhat in awe of many other Signers.

Appointed by President George Washington in 1789 to be an Associate Justice of the United States Supreme Court.

Although a slave owner himself, Blair signed the **Virginia Association**, of June 27, 1774, which banned any further importing of slaves from England.

Heroic Deed: Refused offer of amnesty from British Governor Gage in June 1775.

Little Known Fact: One of 12 Signers of the *Constitution* who owned slaves. The others were Bassett, Blount, Butler, Carroll, Jenifer,

Madison, both Pinckneys, Rutledge, Spaight and Washington.

Price Paid for Signing: All the Signers, including Blair, suffered monetary losses because of their connection with the cause. Some were brought to the brink of financial ruin, or even worse, abject poverty.

William Blount
(1749 – 1800)

Heritage: English. Born on grandfather's Rosefield estate near Windsor, Bertie County, North Carolina. Great grandson of Thomas Blount who immigrated to Virginia from England around 1660.

Religion: Devout Christian. Episcopal, Presbyterian.

Education: Apparently had an excellent education. Studies undertaken mostly at home, primarily by the finest of private tutors. He was also an avid reader and did this whenever time permitted.

Marriage: Wed Mary Grainger [Granger] on February 12, 1778.

Children: Six children, all of whom reached adulthood. Three sons – Eliza, William and Richard; three daughters –Anne, Barbara and Mary Louisa.

Interesting Highlights: One of 39 men who signed the *Constitution*.

Was a close personal friend of George Washington.

Reluctantly affixed his signature to the Constitution in order as he said, to make it *"the unanimous act of the States in Convention."*

Described by a fellow Signer as: "No speaker, nor does he possess any of those talents that make men shine."

Elected as one of Tennessee's first Senators under the new U.S. Constitution. Served in this capacity from 1796 to 1797.

Expelled from the U.S. Senate on a conspiracy charge on July 8, 1797, by a vote of 25 to 1.

Impeached by the House of Representatives but all charges were dropped by the Senate in 1798.

Heroic Deed: Volunteered to serve during the Revolutionary War in the North Carolina militia as well as the 3rd Regimental Continental troops.

Refused an offer of amnesty from British Governor Gage in June 1775.

Little Known Fact: One of the 12 Signers of the *Constitution* who owned slaves. The others Bassett, Blair, Butler, Carroll, Jenifer, Madison, Charles and Charles Cotesworth Pinckney, Rutledge, Spaight and Washington

Price Paid for Signing: All the Signers, including Blount, suffered monetary losses because of their connection with the cause. Some were brought to the brink of financial ruin, or even worse, abject poverty.

David Brearly
(1745 – 1790)

Heritage: Born in Spring Grove, New

Jersey, near Trenton. Descendant of a Yorkshire, England, family. They emigrated from England to the Colonies around 1680.

Religion: Devout Christian. Compiler of the **PROTESTANT EPISCOPAL PRAYER BOOK.**

Education: Private tutors handled most schooling. Attended the College of New Jersey (presently Princeton). Another of our Founding Fathers who studied under the highly influential Reverend John Witherspoon.

Marriage: Twice married. Wed Elizabeth Mullen around 1767, a young woman from a prominent, well-to-do family. She died. R and left him a remarried in 1783, this time to the lovely and quite wealthy Elizabeth Higbee.

Children: Unknown.

Interesting Highlights: 42-years old delegate to the *Constitutional Convention* held in Philadelphia for a four month period between May 25 to September 17, 1787.

One of 39 men who signed the *Constitution*.

Although not a leading figure during the Constitutional Convention, he religiously attended every session.

Once arrested by the British and charged with *"high treason,"* because of his outspokenness regarding the cause of liberty and independence

When the *Constitution* was ratified by New Jersey in 1788, he was the man who presided over that State Convention.

Served as a Presidential Elector in 1789.

Rewarded by President Washington for his loyalty in 1789. Appointed to his last government position before he died – that of Federal District Judge.

Heroic Deed: Refused offer of amnesty from British Governor Gage in June 1775.

Little Known Fact: Fought courageously under General George Washington as a Colonel in the Continental Army.

Price Paid for Signing: All the Signers, including Brearly, suffered monetary losses because of their connection with the cause. Some were brought to the brink of financial ruin, or even worse, abject poverty.

Jacob Broom
(1752 – 1810)

Heritage: Swedish. Born in Wilmington, Delaware. Father immigrated to America from Sweden sometime in the mid-1700s.

Religion: Devout Christian. Lay leader at the Old Swedes Church.

Education: Primarily tutored at home by his mother. Attended the local Old Academy. Studied surveying on his own. An avid reader.

Marriage: Wed Rachel Pierce in 1773 when he was 21-years of age. Very little is known about her.

Children: Eight.

Interesting Highlights: Delegate to the Constitutional Convention in Philadelphia, convened from May 25 to September 17, 1787.

One of 39 men who signed the *Constitution*.

Wasn't a prominent patriot as were so many of the other Signers.

Never absent from any session of the Constitutional Convention.

Offered his opinion in some debates, but overall had little to say.

Said to be an extremely shy man. Appeared to be uncomfortable in the presence of the other wealthier, better-educated delegates.

Apparently made no significant contributions during the Convention.

Participated in the effort to get the *Constitution* ratified in Delaware.

Became first Postmaster in Wilmington, Delaware from 1790 to 1792.

Successful businessman. But he was in the import-export trade, owned a cotton mill and ran a machine shop.

Probably the most obscure Signer of the *Constitution*.

Heroic Deed: Refused offer of amnesty from British Governor Gage in June 1775.

Little Known Fact: His claim to fame, other than for signing the *Constitution*, was to draw maps for General Washington prior to the Battle of Brandywine.

Price Paid for Signing: All the Signers, including Broom, suffered monetary losses because of their connection with the cause. Some were brought to the brink of financial ruin, or even worse, abject poverty

Pierce Butler
(1744 – 1822)

Heritage: Irish. Born in Ireland. Family immigrated to America from Ireland sometime in the late 1600s or early 1700s. Member of the British hereditary aristocracy,

Religion: Devout Christian. Learned to read using a *Bible* in the home. Active member of Christ's Church.

Education: Much of his early education was obtained at home with the finest available tutors. Also attended prestigious private schools.

Marriage: Wed Mary Middleton in 1771. She was the daughter of a wealthy South Carolina planter and prominent Colonial leader.

Children: One daughter who grew up and married a doctor.

Interesting Highlights: Played a major role at the Constitutional Convention.

One of the Constitutional Convention's most aristocratic members.

One of 39 men who signed the *Constitution*.

One of four Signers of the *Constitution* who was born in Ireland. The others were Fitzsimmons, McHenry and Paterson.

Personally contributed money and supplies to help the Continental Army under General Washington.

Father-in-law was President of the First Continental Congress that convened on September 5, 1774, at Carpenter's Hall in Philadelphia.

Brother-in-law, Arthur Middleton, was a delegate to the Second Continental Congress that convened on May 10, 1775, at the State House in Philadelphia.

Middleton also signed the *Declaration of Independence.*

Owned 10,000+-acre plantation in coastal region of South Carolina.

Owned fleet of coastal ships for use in his prosperous export business.

A detachment of his unit fired *"the shots heard 'round the world,"* in 1770 at what became famous as ***"The Boston Massacre."***

Heroic Deed: Refused offer of amnesty from British Governor Gage in June 1775

Little Known Fact: One of 12 Signers of the *Constitution* who owned slaves. The others were Bassett, Blair, Blount, Daniel Carroll, Jenifer, Madison, both Pinckneys, Rutledge, Spaight and Washington.

Price Paid for Signing: All the Signers, including Butler, suffered monetary losses because of their connection with the cause. Some were brought to the brink of financial ruin, or even worse, abject poverty

Daniel Carroll
(1730 – 1796)

Heritage: Irish descent. Born in Upper Marlboro, Maryland. Family emigrated from

Ireland to America sometime in the late 1600s or early 1700s.

Religion: Devout Christian. Roman Catholic. See quote below.

Education: Born to a wealthy family, he was sent from age 12 to 18 to Flanders. There he was to study under the Jesuits at St. Omers (1742 – 1748). Prior to this he had been thoroughly home schooled with only the finest tutors.

Marriage: Wed Eleanor Carroll around 1749 or 1750. She was believed to be the first cousin of Charles Carroll of Carrollton.

Children: Not known.

Interesting Highlights: Attended the Constitutional Convention held in Philadelphia for four months from May 25 and September 17, 1777.

Spoke more than 20 times during the debates over the *Constitution*.

One of the 39 men to sign the *Constitution*.

One of two Roman Catholics to sign the *Constitution*. The other Signer was Thomas Fitzsimmons of Pennsylvania.

One of five men to sign both the *Constitution* and the *Articles of Confederation*. The others were Dickinson, the two Morrises and Sherman.

One of the wealthiest Signers of the *Constitution*. Others were Jenifer and Mifflin. The richest was probably Robert Morris and George Washington.

Older brother, John, became first Roman Catholic bishop in America.

Voted favorably for moving the nation's Capitol to Washington, D.C. (District of Columbia) on the bank of the Potomac River.

Heroic Deed: Strongly supported the *Declaration*. Daniel Carroll knew that should the struggle for independence fail, an ignominious death by hanging would most certainly be his punishment.

Refused an offer of amnesty from British Governor Gage in June 1775.

Little Known Fact: One of 12 Signers of the *Constitution* who owned slaves. The others were Bassett, Blair, Blount, Butler, Jenifer, Madison, both Pinckneys, Rutledge, Spaight and Washington.

Price Paid for Signing: All the Signers, including Carroll, suffered monetary losses because of their connection with the cause. Some were brought to the brink of financial ruin, or even worse, abject poverty.

George Clymer
(1739 – 1813)

Heritage: English. Born in Philadelphia. Father immigrated to America from Bristol, England, sometime early in the 1700s.

Religion: Devout Christian. See quote below.

Education: Received excellent education through private

tutors as a child and young man. Attended the College of Philadelphia (presently the University of Pennsylvania).

Marriage: Was 26 when he wed Elizabeth Meredith in March of 1765. Said to be a "handsome woman" from a prominent Philadelphia family. She was the daughter of his business partner.

Children: Eight. Three died during childhood. Those who lived were Henry, George, Meredith, Margaret and Nancy.

Interesting Highlights: He and George Ross were appointed to be delegates to the Continental Congress in 1776. They were sent to take the place of two Pennsylvania delegates who declined to cast their vote in favor of the *Declaration of Independence*.

One of 56 men to sign the *Declaration of Independence*. Hancock was the *only* one to sign on July 4, 1776. Another 49 signed on August 2. Six signed at a later date – they were Richard Henry Lee, Gerry, McKean, Thorton, Wolcott and Wythe.

Heroic Deed: Signing the *Declaration*. George Clymer knew that should the struggle for independence fail, an ignominious death by hanging would most certainly be his punishment.

Refused an offer of amnesty from British Governor Gage in 1775.

Little Known Fact: Given command of a large volunteer militia group in 1774 when it appeared to be inevitable that military action would be necessary to gain independence from England.

Orphaned in 1740 when only one year old. Raised by wealthy uncle who left him a sizable amount of land and money.

Price Paid for Signing: Most of his property was destroyed. Home sacked and pillaged. Everything movable was either stolen or burned in the front yard as his family watched. Horses, cattle and other animals were either confiscated to feed the soldiers, or killed on the spot.

All the Signers, including Clymer, suffered great monetary losses because of their connection with the cause. Some were brought to the brink of financial ruin, or even worse, abject poverty.

Jonathan Dayton
(1760 – 1824)

Heritage: English. Born in Elizabethtown (presently Elizabeth), New Jersey. Family emigrated to America from England sometime in the late 1600s or early 1700s.

Religion: Devout Christian.

Education: Primarily tutored by mother. Ended up with a good, well-rounded education. Attended the College of New Jersey (presently Princeton). Graduated in 1776.

Marriage: Wed a woman named Susan Williamson. Wedding date unknown.

Children: Two daughters.

Interesting Highlights: Religiously attended every session of the Constitutional Convention.

One of 39 men who signed the *Constitution*.

One of three men in their twenties to sign the *Constitution*. Others were Spaight and Charles Pinckney.

Joined Continental Army upon graduation from college.

Captain in the Continental Army at the age of only 19.

Served in the Continental Army under the famed French General Lafayette as well as his father, General Elias Dayton.

Took part in the Battle of Yorktown and other military engagements.

Captured by British forces and held in prison for a period of time.

City of Dayton, Ohio, was named after this great American patriot.

Charged with treason because of close association with Aaron Burr's attempt to create own empire. indicted but never prosecuted.

Served in U.S. Senate under the new *Constitution* from 1779 to 1805.

Heroic Deed: Refused an offer of amnesty from British Governor Gage in June 1775.

Little Known Fact: Youngest Signer of the Constitution at 26 years of age. The oldest Signer was 81-year old Benjamin Franklin.

Price Paid for Signing: All the Signers, including Dayton, suffered monetary losses because of their connection with the cause. Some were brought to the brink of financial ruin, or even worse, abject poverty.

John Dickinson
(1732 – 1808)

Heritage: English. Father was prosperous farmer who immigrated to America from England sometime between the late 1600s and early 1700s.

Religion: Devout Christian.   See quote below.

Education: Private tutors most of his childhood and as a young adult. Studied law in 1750 under prominent attorney, John Moland in Philadelphia. Sailed to England in 1753 to continue studies at London's Middle Temple.

Marriage: Wed Mary Morris, daughter of an wealthy businessman in 1770.

Children: One daughter.

Interesting Highlights: Delegate to the First Continental Congress that convened on September 5, 1774, at Carpenter's Hall in Philadelphia.

Delegate to the Second Continental Congress that convened on May 10, 1775, at the State House in Philadelphia. While in attendance he wrote "**The Causes of Taking Up Arms.**"

Met with other delegates to the Second Continental Congress less than two months before the vote for the *Declaration of Independence*. He suggested that all delegates be required to repeat the oath quoted below before they would be allowed to be seated and take part in the congressional sessions.

One of 39 signers of the *Constitution.*

One of five men who signed both the *Constitution* and the *Articles of Confederation.* Others were Daniel Carroll, Gouverneur and Robert Morris, and Roger Sherman.

One of the first patriots in the Colonies to advocate using force against England in order to gain independence.

Heroic Deed: Enthusiastically supporting the *Declaration.* John Dickinson knew that should the struggle for independence fail, an ignominious death by hanging would most certainly be his punishment.

Refused an offer of amnesty from British Governor Gage in June 1775.

Little Known Fact: Only man to not personally affix his name to the Constitution. Illness prevented him from being there at the time. He thereby authorized another delegate and close friend, George Read, to sign his name on the grand document.

Price Paid for Signing: All the Signers, including Dickinson, suffered monetary losses because of their connection with the cause. Some were brought to the brink of financial ruin, or even worse, abject poverty.

William Few

(1748 – 1828)

Heritage: English. Born on a farm near Baltimore, Maryland. Descendant of Quaker farmers who had immigrated to America from England sometime during the 1680s. First settled in Pennsylvania.

Religion: Devout Christian. Methodist.

Education: Farming left little time for formal schooling. Briefly attended local school run by a traveling teacher in 1760. This provided a rudimentary education. Had a lifelong love of reading and was primarily self-educated this way. Also found time to study law and become an attorney.

Marriage: Wed Catherine Nicholson on an unknown date.

Children: Three daughters.

Interesting Highlights: Delegate to the Constitutional Convention held in Philadelphia from May 25 to September 17, 1787.

Missed majority of the sessions during the Convention.

Was never known to make a speech or enter into any debates during sessions of the Convention..

One of 39 men who signed the *Constitution*.

Delegate to the Continental Congress from 1780 to 1788.

Commanded a company in the Georgia militia.

Frequently skirmished with British units and eventually forced the enemy to withdraw and abandon Augusta, Georgia.

Heroic Deed: Refused offer of amnesty from British Governor Gage in June 1775.

Little Known Fact: Few, along with his brothers and father joined the *"regulators"* in 1771. This was a group that vigorously opposed the Royal Governor. His brother was captured by the British forces and unceremoniously hanged from the closest tree. As a result, the rest of the family fled to Georgia.

Price Paid for Signing: Family was forced to flee when the vengeful British totally destroyed their farm. Everything was taken from the house, piled in front, and burned. Then the pillaged house was totally destroyed, farm animals killed and crops laid waste.

All Signers, including William Few, suffered monetary losses because of their connection with the cause. Some were brought to the brink of financial ruin, or even worse, abject poverty.

Thomas Fitzsimons
(1741 -- 1811)

Heritage: Irish.   Born in Ireland. Immigrated to America from Ireland in 1760 when only 19-years old.

Religion: Devout Christian. Roman Catholic.

Education: All that is known is that an adequate education was provided for him before his father died in America. Mostly tutoring by the best available teachers.

Marriage: Wed Catherine Meade in 1761. She was daughter of a wealthy and prominent Philadelphia businessman.   As a result of this union, he soon after went into business with one of Catherine's brothers.

Children: Not known.

Interesting Highlights: Attended the Constitutional Convention religiously and seldom missed a session.

Apparently made no significant contributions during the *Constitutional Convention* insofar as in the development of the document.

One of 39 men who signed the *Constitution*.

Called the Constitution he helped devise *"a treasure to posterity."*

One of two Roman Catholics who signed the *Constitution*. The other Catholic signer was Daniel Carroll of Maryland.

One of four Signers of the *Constitution* who was born in Ireland. The others were Butler, McHenry and Paterson.

Commanded a Pennsylvania militia group in 1776 and 1777.

Fought against the British during the Revolutionary War at the Battle of Trenton, and later in defense of Philadelphia.

His integrity impressed James Madison.

Donated a large part of his fortune to help the independence movement.

Helped Robert Morris organize the banking facilities used to support the Continental Army and Navy in the final years of the Revolutionary war

Heroic Deed: Refused an offer of amnesty from British Governor Gage in June 1775.

Little Known Fact: Soon after marriage, he soon after went into business with a brother of his wife, George Mead (the grandfather of the famous Civil War General).

Price Paid for Signing: All the Signers, including Fitzsimmons, suffered monetary losses because of their connection with the cause. Some were brought to the brink of financial ruin, or even worse, abject poverty.

Benjamin Franklin
(1706 – 1790)

Heritage: English. Born in Boston. Father immigrated in 1682 to America from England and settled in Massachusetts.

Religion: Christian. A Puritan.

Education: Could never afford private tutoring or prestigious schools. Read and studied on his own extensively. Taught himself five languages.

Marriage: Took a common law wife in September of 1730. She was Deborah Read, a 25-year old Philadelphia widow. Franklin was 24 at the time. Some sources say they were formally married, others dispute this.

Children: They had two children out of wedlock. Sarah was born in 1774. Their son died as an infant.

Interesting Highlights: The oldest Signer of the *Declaration of Independence* at 70, and of the *Constitution* at 83.

Founder of the University of Pennsylvania.

Developed the first street lights in Philadelphia.

Organized the first postal system in America and was Deputy Postmaster General of the Colonies (1737-1752).

Organized the first volunteer fire department in America.

Was the fifteenth of seventeen children in his family.

Made a motion that Congress be opened each day with a prayer.

Last official act was making a recommendation to Congress that they formally abolish slavery.

Little Known Fact: Sickly and frail when he signed the *Constitution*, he had to be carried in a chair from his home to the sessions of the Constitutional Convention by prisoners incarcerated in the city jail.

All the Signers, including Franklin, suffered monetary losses because of their connection with the cause. Some were brought to the brink of financial ruin, or even worse, abject poverty.

Nicholas Gilman
(1755 – 1814)

Heritage: English. Born in Exter, New Hampshire. Second son in family of eight. Parents immigrated to America from England in the late 1600s or early 1700s.

Religion: Christian. See quote below.

Education: attended various local schools. Mother tutored (home schooled) him as a child and young adult. Voracious reader. Never had either the time or the money to attend college. Had to work as a clerk for his father.

Marriage: Never married. Was lifelong bachelor.

Interesting Highlights: One of 39 men who signed the *Constitution*.

Had no experience in public speaking or debating.

Never made a speech or entered into a debate during sessions of the Constitutional Convention due to his inherent shyness.

Played important role and spent much time to obtain ratification of the new *United States Constitution* in New Hampshire.

One of three Signers of the *Constitution* who were bachelors. The others were Abraham

Baldwin and Daniel of St. Thomas Jenifer. Only two bachelors signed the *Declaration of Independence* – Joseph Hewes and Caesar Rodney. Served as a delegate to the Continental Congress (1785-1787) but didn't bother attending any sessions.

President of the Continental Congress from June 1786 to January 1787.

Served in House of Representatives under the new *Constitution* from 1789 to 1797.

Played minor role in developing the *Constitution*, but a major role in shepherding it through the Continental Congress.

Heroic Deed: Refused an offer of amnesty from British Governor Gage in June 1775.

Little Known Fact: Served throughout the Revolutionary War as a Captain in the Continental Army.

Price Paid for Signing: All the Signers, including Gilman, suffered monetary losses because of their connection with the cause. Some were brought to the brink of financial ruin, or even worse, abject poverty.

Nathaniel Gorham
(1738 – 1796)

Heritage: English. Born in Charlestown, Massachusetts. Family came to America from England sometime in the late 1600s or early 1700s.

Religion: Devout Christian.

Education: No formal schooling. The only education he received was from tutoring at home by various family members. No college.

Marriage: Wed lovely Rebecca Call in 1763.

Children: Nine.

Interesting Highlights: Began career in government as a notary public in Boston.

Elected to Colonial Legislature and served from 1771 to 1775.

Delegate to the Constitutional Convention.

Influential at the Convention. Spoke often during debates.

One of 39 men who signed the *Constitution*.

Delegate to the State Constitutional Convention in Massachusetts. Firmly supported ratification of the United States *Constitution*.

Took his job as a delegate very seriously and was never known to miss a session of the Continental Congress.

Despite humble beginnings, he rose to become President of the Continental Congress from June of 1786 to January of .1787.

Heroic Deed: Refused an offer of amnesty from British Governor Gage in June 1775.

Little Known Fact: From humble beginnings. Quit his job after apprenticing six years with local merchant. Went into business for himself. Became one of the richest and most successful businessmen and landowners in Massachusetts.

Bankrupt when he died at the age of 58-years.

Price Paid for Signing: In retaliation for his deeds as a patriot, the British destroyed much of his land during the Revolutionary War. They burned him home and devastated his property.

Alexander Hamilton
(1757 -- 1804)

Heritage: Scottish-English-French. Born in the West Indies, the illegitimate son from a common law marriage. His mother was a planter's daughter of English-French descent. His father was a Scottish traveling salesman who deserted his family.

Religion: Christian.

Education: Basic education came about through tutoring by a Presbyterian clergyman. A brilliant thinker, he taught himself to speak and write fluent French. Studied law on his own. Opened a practice in Albany, New York. Attended King's College (presently Columbia University) in 1773 at the age of 16, but his formal schooling was interrupted by the Revolutionary War.

Marriage: Married Elizabeth Schuyler in 1780. She came from a filthy rich and politically powerful New York family.

Children: Eight children were born of this union.

Interesting Highlights: One of 39 men who signed the *Constitution*.

Unhappy as a child in the West Indies, he ran away and immigrated to America in 1772 when only 15-years of age.

Upon his arrival in the Colonies, he enthusiastically joined in the fight for American independence.

Although of modest origins, Hamilton rose to become one of the young Republic's brightest stars.

One of General Washington's closest friends and most trusted advisors during the Revolutionary War.

Served in every major campaign during the War in 1776 and 1777.

Hamilton's life ended tragically when mortally wounded in duel with Aaron Burr, a man who was his deadly political adversary and a person he despised. Hamilton was heard to mutter: *"I have lived like a man, but I die as a fool."* He died in his late forties while in the prime of life.

Quotable Quote: *"The best we can hope for concerning the people at large is that they be properly armed."*

Heroic Deed: Refused an offer of amnesty from British Governor Gage in June 1775.

Little Known Fact: Only man to sign the *Constitution* who was born in the West Indies.

Price Paid for Signing: All the Signers, including Hamilton, suffered monetary losses because of their connection with the cause. Some were brought to the brink of financial ruin, or even worse, abject poverty.

Jared Ingersoll
(1749 – 1822)

Heritage: English. Born in New Haven, Connecticut. Father was a British official in the

Colonies and later a prominent loyalist. Family immigrated to America from England in the late 1600s or early 1700s.

Religion: Devout Christian. Brought up in a Christian home where *Bible* readings were commonplace. Regularly attended the Presbyterian Church in Philadelphia.

Education: Privately tutored as a child and young adult. Graduated from Yale in 1766. Sent to England in 1773 to study law in London's Middle Temple until 1776. Completed studies at London's Middle Temple in 1776 and then toured Europe for two more years in order to avoid serving in the Revolutionary War.

Marriage: Married Elizabeth Pettit in 1781. No more is known about this union.

Children: Three. Little or nothing is known about any of them.

Interesting Highlights: Elected to be delegate to the Continental Congress (1780-1781).

Religiously attended every session of the Constitutional Convention held in Philadelphia for about four months from May 25 to September 17, 1787.

Although a lawyer who was known to be a good debater, Ingersoll rarely spoke during the proceedings.

One of 39 men who signed the *Constitution*.

Believed that the election of Thomas Jefferson as President in 1780 to be a terrible blow for the new nation and he called it a "great subversion."

Unsuccessfully ran for Vice-President in 1812 on the Federalist ticket.

Heroic Deed: In June of 1775, British Governor Gage made a desperate attempt to stem the tide of the blossoming independence movement in the Colonies. Amnesty was offered to *every* Colonist with the exception of Samuel Adams and John Hancock, who would lay down his arms and swear their unwavering loyalty to the Crown. To their credit, not one patriot, including Jared Ingersoll, turn coated and accepted the pardon.

Little Known Fact: Was attorney who represented William Blount when he was impeached in 1779.

Price Paid for Signing: All the Signers, including Ingersoll, suffered monetary losses because of their connection with the cause. Some were brought to the brink of financial ruin, or even worse, abject poverty.

Daniel of St. Thomas Jenifer (1723 – 1790)

Heritage: Swedish-English. Born near Port Tobacco in Charles County, Maryland. Family emigrated to America from Sweden and England sometime late in the 1600s or early in the 1700s.

Religion: Devout Christian.

Education: Family utilized services of finest private tutors during childhood and as young adult. Very bright young man. Insatiably read books. Was self-taught in many areas of knowledge.

Marriage: Never married. Was wealthy, aristocratic bachelor.

Children: None.

Interesting Highlights: Delegate to the Continental Congress from 1778 to 1782.

Little known about his childhood other than he grew up on Stepney, the family estate near Annapolis.

A popular figure among the political leaders of his day.

Became close, personal friend of George and Martha Washington.

Initially reluctant to support the Colonial independence movement.

Seldom missed a session of the Constitutional Convention.

On the shy, retiring side, he seldom spoke during debates.

Made little impact on the outcome of the Constitutional Convention.

One of 39 men who signed the *Constitution*.

One of three Signers of the *Constitution* who were lifelong bachelors. The others were Baldwin and Gilman. Two bachelors signed the Declaration of Independence. They were Joseph Hewes of North Carolina and Caesar Rodney of Delaware..

Among the wealthiest Signers of the *Constitution*. Others were Carroll and Mifflin. The richest were probably Robert Morris and Washington.

Heroic Deed: Refused an offer of amnesty from British Governor Gage in June 1775.

Little Known Fact: One of 12 Signers of the *Constitution* who owned slaves. The others were Bassett, Blair, Blount, Butler, Carroll, Madison, both Pinckneys, Rutledge, Spaight and Washington.

Price Paid for Signing: All the Signers, including Jenifer, suffered monetary losses because of their connection with the cause. Some were brought to the brink of financial ruin, or even worse, abject poverty.

William Samuel Johnson (1727 – 1819)

Heritage: English-Scottish. Born in Stratford, Connecticut. Family immigrated to America from England sometime late in 1600s or early 1700s.

Religion: Devout Christian. Father was a highly regarded and well-known Anglican minister.

Education: Privately tutored. Graduated from Yale at 17-years of age. Later awarded honorary Masters Degree by Harvard as well as Oxford University in 1765 and his Doctorate in 1766.

Marriage: Twice married. Wed Anne Beach in 1749. This union added immensely to his wealth. Retired in 1800, a short time after Anne died. Soon thereafter remarried, this time to Mary Brewster Beach, a relative of his first wife, Anne.

Children: Samuel and Anne had six sons and five daughters. Most died as infants or young children. No children were born to the second union.

Interesting Highlights: One of 39 men who signed the *Constitution*.
Delegate to the First Continental Congress that convened on September 5, 1774, at Carpenter's Hall in Philadelphia.

Initially refused to take an active part in any of the proceedings.

Found it impossible to take sides regarding the *Declaration* and the oncoming war because of his many friends residing in England.

Delegate to the Constitutional Convention that met for a four month period in Philadelphia from May 25 to September 17, 1787.

Arrived at the Constitutional Convention on June 2, 1787, and never missed a session.

An officer in the Connecticut militia during the 1750s.

One of the most highly educated signers of the *Constitution*.

Sent to mediate with General Gage in an effort to stop the fighting and bloodshed. The mission failed because of the General's obstinacy.

Quotable Quote: A few of his words selected for inclusion in the *Constitution* of Connecticut were: *"The people of this State ... by the Providence of God hath the sole and exclusive* *right of governing themselves as a free, sovereign, and independent State."*

Heroic Deed: Refused an offer of amnesty from British Governor Gage in June 1775.

Little Known Fact: Son of the first President of King's College, Samuel Johnson (presently Columbia University in New York City).

Price Paid for Signing: All the signers, including Johnson, suffered monetary losses because of their connection with the cause. Some were brought to the brink of financial ruin, or even worse, abject poverty.

Rufus King
(1755 – 1827)

Heritage: English. Born in Scarboro, Massachusetts. Family emigrated to America from England. Son of prosperous farmer-merchant.

Religion: Devout Christian.

Education: Educated in local schools until he was 12. Privately tutored from then to adulthood. Attended highly regarded Drummer Academy in South Bayfield, Massachusetts. Graduated from Harvard in 1777.

Marriage: Wed Mary Alsop in 1786. She was the daughter of an extremely wealthy new York businessman.

Children: Several offspring, but actual number is unknown.

Interesting Highlights: One of the youngest men elected to be a delegate to the Constitutional Convention (age 32) that convened in Philadelphia for four month period from May 25 to September 17, 1787.

One of the 39 signers of the *Constitution*.

Early opponent of slavery in the Colonies.

Tried to have slavery abolished in 1785 with the assistance of Ellery.

Served during Revolutionary War as aide to unknown general.

Ran for President in 1816. Was soundly defeated by James Madison, fellow Signer of the *Constitution*.

Heroic Deed: Strongly supporting the *Declaration*. Rufus King knew that should the struggle for independence fail, an ignominious death by hanging would most certainly be his punishment.

Refused an offer of amnesty from British Governor Gage in June 1775.

Little Known Fact: King strongly objected to setting a date for Congress to meet each year. He felt this wasn't necessary and possibly even dangerous. His exact words were: *"A great vice in our system is that of legislating too much."* Were not his words prophetic?

Price Paid for Signing: All the Signers, including King, suffered monetary losses because of their connection with the cause. Some were brought to the brink of financial ruin, or even worse, abject poverty.

John Langdon
(1741 – 1819)

Heritage: English. Born in or near Portsmouth, New Hampshire. Descendant of a

family that immigrated to America from England prior to 1660. They were among the first to settle at the mouth of the Piscataqua River (today better known as Portsmouth, a major New England seaport).

Religion: Devout Christian. Founder and first President of the **New Hampshire** *Bible* **Society**. His goal was to make certain that every home in New Hampshire had a *Bible*.

Education: Primarily educated at a local school. Some tutoring at home by his mother.

Private tutors hired as necessary. Never attended college.

Marriage: Wed Elizabeth Sherburne in 1777. Nothing is known about their marriage.

Children: One daughter. May have had more, but this is unknown.

Interesting Highlights: Paid own way as well as Gilman's in order that they could attend the Constitutional Convention as official delegates. New Hampshire couldn't or wouldn't pay the expenses of their delegates.

Known to have spoken at least 20 times during the debates.

One of 39 men who signed the *Constitution*.

Heroically fought during the Revolutionary War as a Colonel in the New Hampshire militia.

Built privateers (ships) to operate against the British fleet.

In command of a militia unit at Saratoga, New York, when British General John Burgoyne surrendered.

Heroic Deeds: Refused an offer of amnesty from British Governor Gage in June 1775.

Key figure when a number of patriots boldly confiscated munitions from the fort in Portsmouth, New Hampshire.

Little Known Fact: Used his own money in 1777 to organize and underwrite the cost of a military expedition led by General John Stark from New Hampshire to join the fight against British General John Burgoyne.

Price Paid for Signing: All the Signers, including Langdon, suffered monetary losses because of their connection with the cause. Some were brought to the brink of financial ruin, or even worse, abject poverty.

William Livingston (1723 – 1790)

Heritage: Scottish-Dutch. Born in Albany, New York, to one of the wealthiest and most

politically powerful families in the Colonies. Descendants emigrated to America from Rotterdam, Holland, sometime during the 1600s.

Religion: Christian. Descendant of a Scots minister. Spent one year as missionary when 14-years old.

Education: Tutored (home schooled) by his maternal grandmother until 14-years of age. Went on to Yale, as did older brother, Philip. Graduated at age 18 in 1741. Studied law in office of a prominent attorney.

Marriage: Wed to a lovely young girl named Susanna French in 1745 before completing his study of law. She was the daughter of a wealthy New Jersey land owner.

Children: Had 13 children.

Interesting Highlights: One of 39 men who signed the *Constitution*.

Delegate to the First Continental Congress that convened on September 5, 1774, in Philadelphia at Carpenter's Hall.

Delegate to the Second Continental Congress that convened on May 10, 1775, in the Philadelphia State House.

Served as a delegate to the Constitutional Convention from May 25 to September 17, 1787.

Instrumental in getting New Jersey to quickly ratify the new *United States Constitution.*

Became the first Governor of New Jersey under the new *Constitution.*

Published the controversial weekly, *The Independent Reflector.*

Heroic Deed: Dropped out of the Second Continental Congress in 1776 to take command of the New Jersey militia as a Brigadier General. Led his troops during the first days of the Revolutionary War.

Refused an offer of amnesty from British Governor Gage in June 1775.

Little Known Fact: His older brother, Philip, was a Signer of the *Declaration of Independence*.

Price Paid for Signing: All the Signers, including Livingston, suffered monetary losses because of their connection with the cause. Some were brought to the brink of financial ruin, or even worse, abject poverty.

James Madison
(1751 – 1836)

Heritage: English. Born to a planter  aristocracy in Port Conway, King George County, Virginia. Descendants immigrated to America from England sometime in the 1600s. May also have Scottish and Welsh relatives.

Religion: Christian. First considered becoming a minister and did postgraduate study in theology.

Education: Home schooled by his mother and tutored by a variety of the best teachers. Also attended a number of prestigious private schools. Graduated from the College of New Jersey (now Princeton)

Marriage: Married Dolly Payne Todd in 1749. She was a widow and 16 years younger than James.

Children: No children of their own, but lovely and vivacious Dolly brought a son to their marriage.

Interesting Highlights: The oldest of 10 children in his family.

A slave owner all of his life, he was an active member of the *American Colonization Society*, a group dedicated to sending all slaves back to Africa.

One of the most influential members of the *Constitutional Convention.* Rarely absent, he almost totally dominated the proceedings.

Deservedly known today *as "The Father of the Constitution."*

His most important contribution as one of our Founding Fathers was his work on the writing of our *Constitution.*

One of 39 men who signed the *Constitution.*

He outlived all other Signers of the *Constitution.*

Collaborated with John Jay and fellow Signer of the *Constitution,* Alexander Hamilton, in writing a series of essays. They were published in newspapers in 1787 and 1788. These writings were later published as a book titled *The Federalist Papers.*

Heroic Deed: When the *Constitution* came up for ratification in Virginia, he had to defend the document against such great patriot orators as Patrick Henry, Richard Henry Lee and George Mason.

Refused an offer of amnesty from British Governor Gage in June 1775.

Little Known Fact: Madison was one of 12 signers of the *Constitution* who owned slaves. The others were Bassett, Blair, Blount, Butler, Daniel Carroll, Jenifer, both Pinckneys, Rutledge, Spaight and Washington.

Price Paid for Signing: All the Signers, including Madison, suffered monetary losses because of their connection with the cause. Some were brought to the brink of financial ruin, or even worse, abject poverty.

James McHenry
(1753 – 1816)

Heritage: Irish.   Born in Ballymena County Antrim, Ireland.   Emigrated by himself from Ireland to America in 1771.   Settled in Philadelphia.

Religion: Devout Christian.   President of the *Pennsylvania Bible Society.*

Education: Highly educated in Ireland. Had only the best private tutors. Studied medicine in Philadelphia under the famed Dr. Benjamin Rush, who later Signed the *Declaration of Independence.*

Marriage: Wed Margaret Allison Caldwell in 1784. Nothing much is known about his wife or their marriage.

Children: Three children, two of whom survived him.

Interesting Highlights: Delegate from Maryland to the Continental Congress from 1783 to 1786.

Captured by British at Fort Washington, New York, late in 1776. Released in prisoner exchange in March of 1778.

Delegate to the Constitutional Convention that met in Philadelphia for a four month period from May 25 to September 17, 1787.

Missed many sessions due to family illness, but was seated when it came time to sign the document.

One of 39 men to sign the *Constitution.*

Pushed hard for ratification of the new *U. S. Constitution* in Maryland.

Served as a surgeon in the Continental Army, first on the staff of Washington, then under Lafayette until 1781.

Elected in 1781 to be the first Senator from Maryland under the new *Constitution*

Washington appointed this trusted friend to be his first Secretary of War.

Heroic Deed: Vigorously supported the *Declaration*. James McHenry knew that should the struggle for independence fail, an ignominious death by hanging would most certainly be his punishment.

Refused an offer of amnesty from British Governor Gage in June 1775.

Little Known Fact: One of four Signers of the *Constitution* who were born in Ireland. The others were Butler, Fitzsimmons and Paterson.

Price Paid for Signing: All the Signers, including McHenry, suffered monetary losses because of their connection with the cause. Some were brought to the brink of financial ruin, or even worse, abject poverty.

Thomas Mifflin
(1744 -- 1780)

Heritage: English. Born in Philadelphia, Pennsylvania, the "Cradle of Liberty". Family immigrated to America from England during the early 1600s.

Religion: Devout Christian. Quaker.

Education: Attended a Quaker school. Later attended the College of Philadelphia (presently University of Pennsylvania. Graduated when only 16-years old.

Marriage: Wed Sarah Morris in 1767. Little more is known about the marriage, except that she wholeheartedly supported her husband's involvement in the independence movement.

Children: Unknown.

Interesting Highlights: Delegate to the Constitutional Convention in 1787 and never missed a session.

Made no significant contributions while at the Convention.

One of 39 men who signed the *Constitution*.

One of the wealthier Signers of the *Constitution*. Others of the wealthy elite included Carroll and Jenifer. The richest men of all were probably Robert Morris and George Washington.

Delegate to the First Continental Congress that convened on September 5, 1774, at Carpenter's Hall in Philadelphia.

Delegate to the Second Continental Congress that convened on May 10, 1775, at the State House in Philadelphia.

Became close friends with Washington after successfully recruiting troops for the Continental Army.

Had strong pacifist beliefs.

Fought in Princeton, Trenton as well as on Long Island.

Heroic Deed: Refused an offer of amnesty from British Governor Gage in June 1775.

Little Known Fact: Expelled from Quaker faith in May of 1775, for joining Continental Army. Was an aide-de-camp to General Washington.

Price Paid for Signing: Lived an affluent life, but was broke when he died at the age of 56. There wasn't even enough money to pay his burial expenses. All of the Signers suffered monetary losses because of their connection with the cause. Some of the others were also brought to the brink of financial ruin, or even worse, abject poverty as was the case with Mifflin.

Gouverneur Morris (1752 – 1816)

Heritage: Born at the Morrisania Estate in Westchester County (now the Bronx), New York. Family emigrated from England to America.

Religion: Devout Christian.

Education: Taught by the best of tutors. Attended a prestigious Huguenot school in New Rochelle. Later attended Kings College (presently Columbia University in New York City). Graduated in 1768 when just 16-years old. Studied law on his own.

Marriage: Wed rather late in life. Married Anne Cary Randolph in 1809 when he was 57-years old. She was from a prominent Virginia family.

Children: One son.

Interesting Highlights: One of 39 men who signed the *Constitution*.

One of five men who signed both the *Constitution* and the *Articles of Confederation*. The others who also signed were Carroll, Dickinson, Robert Morris and Sherman.

Very close friend of George Washington.

Appointed by President Washington to replace Thomas Jefferson as Minister to France (1792-1794).

He, along with Robert Livingston and John Jay, were the three men most responsible for the development of New York's first *Constitution*.

Served in the Pennsylvania militia in 1776.

One of the wittiest and most brilliant members of the Constitutional Convention. Spoke often and humorously,
Responsible for coming up with the idea of using the dollar as the basis for American money.

Wrote the final draft of the *Constitution*.

Originator of the phrase: *"We the People of the United States."*

Older half-brother, Lewis, had the distinction of being one of the Signers of the *Declaration of Independence*.

Heroic Deed: Refused an offer of amnesty from British Governor Gage in June 1775.

Little Known Fact: Lost one leg in a childhood carriage accident.

Penalty Paid for Signing: All the Signers, including Morris, suffered monetary losses because of their connection with the cause. Some were brought to the brink of financial ruin, or even worse, abject poverty.

Robert Morris
(1733 – 1806)

Heritage: English. His father, a Liverpool merchant, immigrated to America sometime in the mid-1700s. A very young Robert was left behind in the care of his grandmother. He was sent for at the age of 13-years.

Religion: Christian. His wife was the daughter of the late venerable Bishop of Pennsylvania.

Education: Brilliant young man. Placed in private school in Philadelphia. Chided by his father for his slowness in learning, Robert replied: *"Why, sir, I have learned all that he could teach me."* The 15-year old was immediately placed in the exporting business. With no more formal education, he became a resounding success and one of the richest men in the Colonies.

Marriage: Wed to Mary White in 1769. He was 35, she 20. Mary was from a wealthy, socially prominent Philadelphia family. She was described as *"tall, graceful and commanding, with a stately dignity of manner."*

Children: Five sons and two daughters. Some sources disagree and say they had only four children – three sons and one daughter.

Interesting Highlights: One of 56 men to sign the *Declaration of Independence.* Hancock was the *only* one to sign on July 4, 1776. Another 49 signed on August 2. Six signed at a later date – they were Richard Henry Lee, Gerry, McKean, Thorton, Wolcott and Wythe.

One of six men to sign both the *Declaration of Independence* and the *Constitution.* The others were Clymer, Franklin, Read, Sherman and Wilson.

One of six to sign both the *Constitution* and *Articles of Confederation.* The others were Daniel Carroll, Dickinson, Gouverneur Morris and Sherman.

One of only two men to sign all three of our nation's basic documents – the *Declaration of Independence, Constitution* and *Articles of Confederation.* The other Signer was Robert Sherman.

Quotable Quote: Astonished and indignant upon hearing about the Battle of Lexington, he said this: *"I vow to dedicate the rest of my life to the cause of freedom."*

Heroic Deed: Signing the *Declaration.* Robert Morris knew that should the struggle for

independence fail, an ignominious death by hanging would most certainly be his punishment.

Refused an offer of amnesty from British Governor Gage in June 1775.

Little Known Fact: One of two Signers of the *Declaration of Independence* who was born in England. The other was Button Gwinnett.

Price Paid for Signing: All the Signers, including Robert Morris, suffered monetary losses because of their connection with the cause. Some were brought to the brink of financial ruin, or even worse, abject poverty.

William Paterson
(1745 – 1806)

Heritage: Irish. Born in County Antrim, Ireland. Family emigrated from Ireland to America in 1747 when he was two years old.

Religion: Devoted Christian. Protestant or Roman Catholic not known.

Education: Much of his youth spent in prestigious private schools. Attended College of New Jersey (presently Princeton). Studied law under the tutelage of Richard Stockton, a prominent attorney who would later affix his signature to the *Declaration of Independence.*

Marriage: Twice married. Wed Cornelia Bell in 1779. She died four years later. Remarried in about two years, this time to Euphemia White.

Children: Three with first wife, Cornelia. She died during childbirth. Not known if children were born to his second union.

Interesting Highlights: One of 39 men who signed the *Constitution.*

One of four Signers of the *Constitution* who were born in Ireland. The others were Butler, Fitzsimmons and McHenry.

One of seven foreign born Signers of the *Constitution,* four of whom were Irish. Those born elsewhere are as follows: Hamilton -- West Indies; Robert Morris – England; and Wilson – Scotland.

Appointed by President George Washington to be an Associate Justice of the Supreme Court. Served from 1793 to 1806.

First man elected to the United States Senate under the new *Constitution.* Served in this capacity from 1789 to 1790.

City of Paterson, New Jersey, was named after him.

Held commission as an officer in the New Jersey militia in 1777.

Heroic Deed: Refused an offer of amnesty from British Governor Gage in June of 1775.

Little Known Fact: Of the 18 members of his class at the College of New Jersey (presently Princeton), 12 went on to become ministers.

Price Paid for Signing: All the Signers, including Paterson, suffered monetary losses because of their connection with the cause. Some were brought to the brink of financial ruin, or even worse, abject poverty.

Charles Pinckney
(1757 – 1824)

Heritage: English. Born in Charleston, South Carolina. Ancestors emigrated to America from England in the early to mid 1600s.

Religion: Devout Christian.

Education: From an aristocratic background, he had only the best tutors and attended only the most prestigious private schools as a youth. Studied law in the office of a prestigious attorney friend of the family.

Marriage: Wed to Mary Eleanor Laurens in 1778. She was the daughter of a wealthy South Carolina merchant and a socialite.

Children: At least three children were born of this union.

Interesting Highlights: One of 39 men who signed the *Constitution*.

Second cousin, Charles Cotesworth, also signed the *Constitution*.

Captain in the South Carolina militia.

Captured by the British when Charleston fell in 1780.

Remained a prisoner of the British invaders until June of 1781.

One of three men in their twenties to sign the *Constitution*. The others were Dayton and Spaight.

Second youngest delegate to the Constitutional Convention.

Often spoke and contributed much to the document's final draft.

Thomas Jefferson's Campaign manager during 1800 when he was running for President of the United States.

Heroic Deed: Served as a lieutenant in the Continental Army under General George Washington. Saw action during the Siege of

Savannah, Georgia, in September and October of 1779.

Refused an offer of amnesty from British Governor Gage in June 1775.

Little Known Fact: One of the 12 Signers of the *Constitution* who owned slaves. The others were Bassett, Blair, Blount, Butler, Carroll, Jenifer, Madison, the other Pinckney, Rutledge, Spaight and Washington.

Price Paid for Signing: All Signers, including Charles Pinckney, suffered monetary losses because of their connection with the cause. Some were brought to the brink of financial ruin, or even worse, abject poverty.

Charles Cotesworth Pinckney (1746 – 1825)

Heritage: English. Born in Charleston, South Carolina. Ancestors immigrated to

America from England in the mid or early or mid-1600s.

Religion: Devout Christian. First President of the Charleston *Bible* Society.

Education: Taken to England by his father when seven in order *"to get a proper education."* Tutored in London and attended the finest British prep schools. Attended Christ Church College in Oxford. Taught by Sir William Blackstone, the foremost legal authority of his day. Then studied for a military career at the prestigious Royal Military Academy of France.

Marriage: Twice married. Wed first wife, Sarah Middleton, in 1773. After Sarah died, he remarried Mary Stead in 1786. Both wives came from wealthy Charleston families of the highest social standing.

Children: None with first wife, Sarah. Three daughters with second wife, Mary. Survived by these daughters.

Interesting Highlights: Washington's trusted aide-de-camp during the War for Independence.

Saw much military action. Participated in the battles fought at Charleston, Brandywine, Germantown and during the Siege of Savannah.

Captured by the British when Charleston fell in 1780. Remained their prisoner until 1782.

Delegate to the Constitutional Convention held in Philadelphia for a four months between May 25 to September 17, 1787.

One of 39 men who signed the *Constitution*.

Younger second cousin, Charles, also signed the *Constitution*.

One of the Constitutional Convention's outstanding leaders.

Heroic Deed: Refused an offer of amnesty from British Governor Gage in June 1775.

Little Known Fact: Charles Cotesworth was one of 12 Signers of the *Constitution* who owned slaves. Others were Bassett, Blair, Blount, Butler, Daniel Carroll, Jenifer, Madison, the other Pinckney, John Rutledge, Spaight and Washington.

Price Paid for Signing: All the Signers, including Pinckney, suffered monetary losses because of their connection with the cause. Some were brought to the brink of financial ruin, or even worse, abject poverty.

George Read
(1733 – 1798)

Heritage: Irish-Welsh. Born in Maryland. Father immigrated to America from Dublin, Ireland, about 1726. Grandfather was wealthy Dublin businessman. Mother was daughter of wealthy Welsh planter.

Religion: Dedicated Christian. Father-in-law, the Reverend George Ross, was pastor for 50 years of the Immanuel Church in New Castle. **Education**: Much early education came from private tutors.

Attended school in Chester, Pennsylvania. Later was able to study under the renown Reverend Francis Alison's most prestigious academy in London, Pennsylvania. Studied law when 15 under the auspices of a prominent Philadelphia attorney.

Marriage: Wed the Gertrude Ross, in 1763. She was the widowed sister of George Ross, fellow Signer of the *Declaration of Independence.*

Children: Six. One daughter. Five sons. Their firstborn died at birth.

Interesting Highlights: Delegate to the Second Continental Congress that convened on May 10, 1775, at the State House in Philadelphia.

One of 56 men to sign the *Declaration of Independence.* Hancock was the *only* one to sign on July 4, 1776. Another 49 signed on August 2. Six signed at a later date – they were Richard Henry Lee, Gerry, McKean, Thorton, Wolcott and Wythe.

One of six men to sign both the *Declaration of Independence* and the *Constitution.* Others were Clymer, Franklin, Morris, Sherman and Wilson.

President of Delaware's Constitutional Convention held in 1776.

Heroic Deed: Signing the *Declaration.* George Read knew that should the struggle for

independence fail, an ignominious death by hanging would most certainly be his punishment.

Refused an offer of amnesty from British Governor Gage in June 1775.

Little Known Fact: Was known to have, on numerous occasions, taken up his musket and marched with the militia to help repel British invaders.

Price Paid for Signing: Wife was forced to flee from their home with the children in tow. Bore many hardships due to the close proximity of the vindictive British Army.

All the Signers, including Read, suffered monetary losses because of their connection with the cause. Some were brought to the brink of financial ruin, or even worse, abject poverty.

John Rutledge (1739 – 1800)

Heritage: Irish. Born near Charleston, South Carolina. Father immigrated to America from Ireland in 1735.

Religion: Devout Christian. Episcopal.

Education: Sent to London for his education. Had only the best private tutors and attended the most prestigious prep schools. Studied law at London's

Middle Temple. Admitted to the English bar in 1760.

Marriage: Wed Elizabeth Grimke sometime in 1763.

Children: 10 children. How many lived past childhood isn't known.

Interesting Highlights: Delegate to the *First Continental Congress* that convened on September 5, 1774, at Carpenter's Hall in Philadelphia.

Delegate to the Second Continental Congress that convened on May 10, 1775, at the State House in Philadelphia.

One of the most influential delegates at the *Constitutional Convention* held in Philadelphia from May 25 and September 17, 1787.

Religiously attended every session of the Convention.

One of the 39 Signers of the *Constitution.*

Younger brother, Edward, was one of the 56 Signers of the *Declaration of Independence.* Hancock was the *only* one to sign the *Declaration* on July 4, 1776. Another 49 signed on August 2. Six signed at a later date – they were Richard Henry Lee, Gerry, McKean, Thorton, Wolcott and Wythe.

Heroic Deed: Vigorously supported the Signing the *Declaration*. John Rutledge knew that should the struggle for independence fail, an ignominious death by hanging would most certainly be his punishment.

Refused offer of amnesty from British Governor Gage in June 1775.

Little Known Fact: One of 12 Signers of the *Constitution* who owned slaves. The others were Bassett, Blair, Blount, Butler, Carroll, Jenifer, Madison, both Pinckney's, Spaight and Washington

Advocated unrestricted slave trade while attending the Constitutional Convention held in Philadelphia from May 25 to September 17, 1787.

Price Paid for Signing: All the Signers, including Rutledge, suffered monetary losses because of their connection with the cause. Some were brought to the brink of financial ruin, or even worse, abject poverty.

Roger Sherman
(1721 – 1793)

Heritage: English descent. Born in Newton, Massachusetts. Parents immigrated to the Colonies from England in the late 1600s or early 1700s.

Religion: John Adams described Sherman as "*...an old Puritan, as honest as an angel and as*

firm in the cause of American Independence as Mount Atlas."

Education: Early formal education extremely limited. Avid reader. Self-taught in

mathematics, astronomy and numerous other subjects. Always kept books open on the workbench while repairing shoes. Studied law by reading books borrowed from local attorneys.

Marriage: Twice married. Wed first wife, Elizabeth Hartwell, in 1749. He was 28. Little is known about Mary. She died 11 years later in 1760. Remarried, this time to Rebecca Prescott. She was 20 and he was 42 at this time.

Children: Seven children born to first union. Eight more born to he and second wife. All but one lived to maturity. Rebecca raised her own eight children as well as the seven born to Roger and Elizabeth.

Interesting Highlights: One of 56 men to sign the *Declaration of Independence*. Hancock was the *only* one to sign on July 4, 1776. Another 49 signed on August 2. Six signed at a later date – they were Richard Henry Lee, Gerry, McKean, Thorton, Wolcott and Wythe.

One of six Signers who also affixed his signature to the *Constitution.* The others were Clymer, Franklin, Robert Morris, Read and Wilson.

Seconded Franklin's motion that congress be opened each day with a prayer.

Made an astounding 128 speeches at the Constitutional Convention.

`**Heroic Deed:** Signing the *Declaration.* Roger Sherman knew that should the struggle for independence fail, an ignominious death by hanging would most certainly be his punishment.

Refused an offer of amnesty from British Governor Gage in June 1775

Little Known Fact: Only man to sign all four of the main founding documents: *Articles of Association* (1774); *Declaration of Independence* (1776); *Articles of Confederation* (1777) and *Constitution* (1787).

Price Paid for Signing: All the Signers, including Sherman, suffered monetary losses because of their connection with the cause. Some were brought to the brink of financial ruin, or even worse, abject poverty.

Richard Dobbs Spaight, Sr. (1758 – 1802)

Heritage: Irish-English. Born to prominent Irish-English family in New Bern, North Carolina. Family immigrated to America from England sometime between the late 1600s and early 1700s.

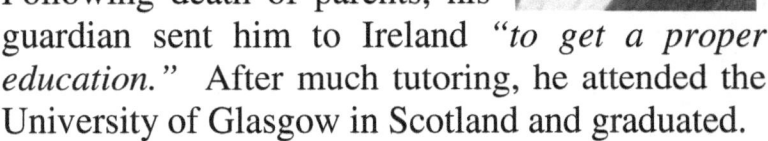

Religion: Dedicated Christian. **Education**: Following death of parents, his guardian sent him to Ireland *"to get a proper education."* After much tutoring, he attended the University of Glasgow in Scotland and graduated.

Marriage: Wed Mary Leach sometime in 1795.

Children: Five.

Interesting Highlights: One of 39 men who signed the *Constitution*.

One of the three youngest Signers of the *Constitution*. The others were Jonathan Dayton and Charles Pinckney.

Helped organize and mobilize of the North Carolina Militia in 1778 and again in 1779. Was an aide to the State militia commander.

Commanded an artillery regiment as a Lieutenant Colonel.

Saw battlefield action in the Revolutionary War during the Battle of Camden, South Carolina, in 1780.

Faithfully attended every session of the Continental Congress and spoke several times during the debates.

Fought ferociously for ratification of the *United States Constitution* in North Carolina where it was exceptionally difficult.

Killed in a senseless duel with a political opponent, federalist John Stanley. His final words could well have been muttered by Alexander Hamilton: *"I have lived like a man, but I die as a fool."* He died in his late forties.

Heroic Deed: Refused an offer of amnesty from British Governor Gage in June 1775.

Little Known Fact: One of 12 Signers of the *Constitution* who owned slaves. Others were Bassett, Blair, Blount, Butler, Daniel Carroll, Jenifer, Madison, the two Pinckneys, Rutledge and Washington.

Penalty Paid for Signing: All the Signers, including Spaight, suffered monetary losses because of their connection with the cause. Some were brought to the brink of financial ruin, or even worse, abject poverty.

George Washington (1732 – 1799)

Heritage: English. Born in Wakefield Plantation, Virginia. The eldest of six children from his father's first marriage. Only 11 when father died.

Religion: Christian. Born and raised in a Godly home. His mother taught him the *Bible* and how to pray. His father taught him to know and to worship God.

Education: Was never formally taught school beyond the elementary level. Privately tutored for the most part.

Marriage: Married Martha Dandridge Custis, an extremely wealthy widow, who had two children from her previous marriage.

Children: He and Martha had no children. He brought up Martha's children as if they were his own.

Interesting Highlights: After the battles of Lexington and Concord, he was selected to be Commander-in-Chief of the Continental Army.

One of 39 men who signed the *Constitution*.

Chosen by the electoral college to be first President of the United States from 1789 to 1797.

Had at least 166 head of prize cattle at Mount Vernon in 1765.

Known to be a workaholic, but was known to take time off to go fishing once in a while. His favorite fish was the shad.

Enjoyed chasing foxes through the woods while on horseback.

Described by Thomas Jefferson as being the most accomplished horseman in America.

Thoroughly denounced the idea that the Continental Army should take over the newly formed government.

Quotable Quote: *"Firearms stand next in importance to the Constitution itself. They are the American people's liberty teeth. ... The very atmosphere of firearms everywhere restrains evil interference."*

Heroic Deed: Refused to consider the offer of important men in the colonies who wished to appoint him king.

Refused an offer of amnesty from British Governor Gage in June 1775.

Little Known Fact: One of 12 Signers of the *Constitution* who owned slaves. The others were Bassett, Blair, Blount, Butler, Daniel Carroll, Jenifer, Madison, both Pinckneys, Rutledge and Spaight.

Price Paid for Signing: All the Signers, including Washington, suffered monetary losses because of their connection with the cause. Much of Washington's extensive fortune was lost due to financial sacrifices and long absences during the war.

Hugh Williamson
(1735 – 1819)

Heritage: Scotch-Irish. Born in West Nottingham, Pennsylvania, the oldest son in a large family. Parents emigrated to America from Scotland and Ireland sometime during the late 1600s.

Religion: Devout Christian. Visited and prayed for the sick as young man. Studied for the ministry. Licensed to preach after father died. Presbyterian clergyman.

Education: Tutored as a child and young adult. Attended a number of prestigious preparatory schools. Entered the first class conducted at the College of Philadelphia (now the University of Pennsylvania). Graduated in 1757. Went abroad in 1764 to study medicine in London, Edinburgh and Utrecht. Received medical degree from the University of Utrecht.

Marriage: Wed to wealthy Maria Apthorpe in 1789.

Children: Had at least two sons. Not much else is known.

Interesting Highlights: Delegate to the Constitutional Convention. One of the 39 men who signed the *Constitution*.

Worked tirelessly for ratification of the *Constitution* in North Carolina.

Witnessed the **Boston Tea Party**.

Brilliant and talented individual. Not only was he a minister at one time, but he was also a physician, scientist and writer.

Professor of Mathematics at the College of Philadelphia (presently the University of Pennsylvania).

Elected in 1789 to the first House of Representatives under the new United States Constitution. Served two terms.

Faithfully attended all sessions of the Constitutional Convention.

James Wilson
(1742 – 1798)

Heritage: Scottish. Born at Carskerdo, near St. Andrews, Scotland. Emigrated to America from Scotland in 1765. Settled in Philadelphia.

Religion: Dedicated Christian.

Education: Tutored by some the finest teachers in Edinburgh. Studied law under John Dickinson, fellow Signer of the *Constitution*.

Awarded honorary Master of Arts degree from the College of Philadelphia (presently University of Pennsylvania) in 1766.

Marriage: Twice married. Wed first wife, Rachel Bird, in 1769 or 1772. She died in 1786. Remarried in 1793, this time to the beautiful Hannah Gray of Boston, daughter of a wealthy merchant.

Children: Rachel bore him five children – four sons and 1 daughter. Hannah had one boy who died as infant.

Interesting Highlights: One of 56 men to sign the *Declaration of Independence*. Hancock was the *only* one to sign on July 4, 1776. Another 49 signed on August 2. Six signed at a later date – they were Richard Henry Lee, Gerry, McKean, Thorton, Wolcott and Wythe.

Extremely active participant at the Constitutional Convention. Known to have spoken 168 times during debates.

One of 39 men to sign the *Constitution.*

One of six men who affixed their signatures to both the *Declaration of Independence* and the *Constitution.* Others were Clymer, Franklin, Robert Morris, Read and Sherman.

One of two Signers of the *Declaration of Independence* born in Scotland. The other was Witherspoon.

Heroic Deed: Signing the *Declaration*. James Wilson knew that should the struggle for independence fail, an ignominious death by hanging would most certainly be his punishment. Refused offer of amnesty from British Governor Gage in June 1775.

Little Known Fact: One of eight Signers of the *Declaration of Independence* who were foreign born. The others were Gwinnett, Lewis, Robert Morris, Smith, Taylor, Thornton and Witherspoon.

Price Paid for Signing: All the Signers, including Wilson, suffered monetary losses because of their connection with the cause. Some were brought to the brink of financial ruin, or even worse, abject poverty. Almost arrested and tossed into debtors prison after the War ended.

12

The Words of Each

Signer of the Constitution

Regarding His Faith

Abraham Baldwin
(1754 – 1807)

Quotable Quote: Believed it to be in the country's best interest *"to support the principles or religion and morality."*

Richard Bassett
(1745 – 1815)

Quotable Quote: Major William Pierce of Georgia wrote character sketches of various delegates to the Constitutional Convention. Here's how he described Bassett: *"A religious enthusiast, lately turned Methodist, who serves his country because it is the will of the people that he should do so. He is a man of plain sense, and has modesty enough to hold his tongue. He is a gentlemanly man, and is in high estimation among Methodists."*

Gunning Bedford
(1747 – 1812)

Quotable Quote: Openly professed his faith *"in God the Father, and in Jesus Christ, His only Son."*

John Blair
(1732 – 1800)

Quotable Quote: On January 11, 1786, Blair's legislation was adopted. It was called the **Virginia Statute of Religious Liberty**: *"Well aware that Almighty God hath created the mind free; that all attempts to influence it by temporal punishments or burdens, or by civil incapacitations ... are a departure from the plan of the Holy Author of our religion."*

William Blount
(1749 – 1800)

Quotable Quote: *"No person who should deny the being of God or the truth of the religion [Christian], or the divine authority of either the Old or New Testaments, or who should hold religious principles incompatible with the freedom and safety of the state, shall be capable of holding any office, or place of trust ...within this state."*

David Brearly
(1745 – 1790)

Quotable Quote: Brearly, Dayton, William Livingston and Paterson are credited with the New Jersey *Constitution*. Here is what they wrote: *"We the people ... grateful to Almighty God for the civil and religious liberty which He hath so long permitted us to enjoy, and looking to Him for a blessing upon our endeavors to secure and transmit the same unimpaired to succeeding* *generations, do ordain and establish this Constitution."*

Jacob Broom
(1752 – 1810)

Quotable Quote: Immigrants from Sweden settled in America and started the first Lutheran Colony. According to Broom, *"the founding of the Colony was based on their belief, and my personal belief as well, in: 'Jesus Christ the Savior of the World'."*

Pierce Butler
(1744 – 1822)

Quotable Quote: *"All men are absolutely dependent upon their Father in Heaven for everything. Each man must find it necessary, in every manner, to conform to the absolute will of his Maker."*

Daniel Carroll
(1730 – 1796)

Quotable Quote: One of the men chosen to develop the Maryland *Constitution*. He wrote in part: *"We the people of the state of Maryland, grateful to Almighty God for our civil and religious liberty ... no other test or qualification ought to be required, on admission to any office ... than such an oath of support and fidelity to this*

state ... and a declaration of a belief in the
Christian religion."

George Clymer
(1739 – 1813)

Quotable Quote: One of the men who developed the Pennsylvania *Constitution*. Clymer spelled out what each member of the legislature must repeat say being seated: *"I do believe in one God, the Creator and Governor of the universe, the rewarder of the good and the punisher of the wicked."*

Jonathan Dayton
(1760 – 1824)

Quotable Quote: Dayton wrote of how members of the Continental Congress responded to Benjamin Franklin's speech calling for prayer each day to open sessions: " *... never did I behold a countenance at once so dignified and delightful as was that of Washington at the close of the address; nor were the members of the convention generally less affected. The words of the venerable Franklin fell upon our ears with weight and authority ... "*

John Dickinson
(1732 – 1808)

Quotable Quote: *"I do profess faith in God the Father, and in Jesus Christ his Eternal*

Son the true God, and in the Holy Spirit, one God blessed for ever more; and I do acknowledge the Holy Scriptures of the Old and New Testaments to be given by Divine Inspiration."

William Few
(1748 – 1828)

Quotable Quote*: "We, the people of Georgia, relying upon the protection and guidance of Almighty God, do ordain and establish this Constitution."*

Thomas Fitzsimons
(1741 -- 1811)

Quotable Quote: One of the men who developed the *Constitution* of Pennsylvania. Fitzsimons insisted on this wording for what legislators must say before being seated: *"I do believe in one God, the Creator and Governor of the universe, the rewarder of the good and the punisher of the wicked."*

Benjamin Franklin
(1706 – 1790)

Quotable Quote: *"In the beginning of the Contest with Great Britain, when we were sensible of the danger we had daily prayer ... for the Divine protection. Our prayers ... were heard, and they were graciously answered."*

Franklin said this on the eve of the American War for Independence in 1774: *"We think it is incumbent upon this people to humble themselves before God on account of their sins. ... so God may be pleased to continue to us the blessings we enjoy, and remove the tokens of His displeasure."*

Nicholas Gilman
(1755 – 1814)

Quotable Quote: Gilman assisted John Langdon in writing New Hampshire's *Constitution*. Here is how he chose to word part of the document: *"Every individual has a natural and inalienable right to worship God according to the dictates of his own conscience, and reason. ... every denomination of Christians ... shall be equally under the protection of the laws. ... And no subordination of any one sect or denomination to another, shall ever be established by law."*

Nathaniel Gorham
(1738 – 1796)

Quotable Quote: Here is the kind of wording he and Rufus King used in drafting the *Constitution* of Massachusetts. Any person elected to the Legislature or a State office must believe in and make this declaration: *"I _____, do declare, that I believe the Christian religion, and* *have firm persuasion of its truth."* In Part 1, Article 11: *"It is the right, as well as the duty, of all men ... to worship the Supreme Being, the Great Creator and Preserver of the Universe. And no subject shall be hurt, molested, or restrained ... for worshipping God in the manner ... most agreeable to the dictates of his own conscience."*

Alexander Hamilton
(1757 -- 1804)

On his deathbed, he said: *"I have a tender reliance on the mercy of the Almighty, through the merits of the Lord Jesus Christ. I am a sinner. I look to him for mercy. Pray for me."*

Jared Ingersoll
(1749 – 1822)

Quotable Quote: One of the men who developed the *Constitution* of Pennsylvania. It clearly spells out what each member of the legislature must say before being seated: *"I do believe in one God, the Creator and Governor of the universe, the rewarder of the good and the punisher of the wicked."*

Daniel of St. Thomas Jenifer
(1723 – 1790)

Quotable Quote: Brave immigrants from Sweden settled in America and started the first Lutheran Colony. According to Jenifer, who was of part Swedish descent: *"I have a very personal belief in and relationship with the Lord Jesus Christ, just as the founders did from the beginning?*

Rufus King
(1755 – 1827)

Quotable Quote: Any person elected to the Legislature or a State office must believe in and make this declaration: *"I _____, do declare, that I believe the Christian religion, and have firm persuasion of its truth."* In Part 1, Article 11: *"It is the right, as well as the duty, of all men ... to worship the Supreme Being, the Great Creator and Preserver of the Universe. And no subject shall be hurt, molested, or restrained ... for worshipping God in the manner ... most agreeable to the dictates of his own conscience."*

John Langdon
(1741 – 1819)

Quotable Quote: In a Thanksgiving proclamation made on October 12, 1785, Governor Langdon said this: *"It ... becomes our indispensable Duty ... to ... acknowledge ... our dependence on the Supreme Ruler of the Universe, but as a people particularly favoured, to testify our Gratitude to the Author of all our Mercies, in the most solemn and public manner."*

William Livingston

(1723 – 1790)

Quotable Quote: Livingston, Dayton, Paterson and Brearly are credited with the New Jersey *Constitution*. Here is what they wrote: *"We the people ... grateful to Almighty God for the civil and religious liberty which He hath so long permitted us to enjoy, and looking to Him for a blessing upon our endeavors to secure and transmit the same unimpaired to succeeding generations, do ordain and establish this Constitution."*

James Madison
(1751 – 1836)

Quotable Quote: *"We have all been encouraged to feel in the guardianship of that Almighty Being, whose power regulates the destiny of nations."*

James McHenry
(1753 – 1816)

Quotable Quote: *" ... the poor cannot be presented by the rich with anything of greater value[than the Bible. ... It is a book ... fitted to every situation in which man can be placed. It is an oracle which reveals to mortals the secrets of heavens and the hidden will of the Almighty."*

Thomas Mifflin
(1744 -- 1780)

Quotable Quote: One of the men who developed the *Constitution* of Pennsylvania. It clearly spells out what each member of the legislature must say before being seated: *"I do believe in one God, the Creator and Governor of the universe, the rewarder of the good and the punisher of the wicked."*

Gouverneur Morris
(1752 – 1816)

Said just before dying: *"Descend towards the grave full of gratitude to the Giver of all good."*

Quotable Quote: *"Religion is the only solid basis of good morals; therefore education should teach the precepts of religion, and the duties of man toward God."*

William Paterson
(1745 – 1806)

Quotable Quote: Paterson, Brearly, Dayton and William Livingston are credited with the development of New Jersey's *Constitution*. Here is what they wrote: *"We the people ... grateful to Almighty God for the civil and religious liberty which He hath so long permitted us to enjoy,* *and looking to Him for a blessing upon our endeavors to secure and transmit the same unimpaired to succeeding generations, do ordain and establish this Constitution."*

Charles Pinckney
(1757 – 1824)

Quotable Quote: Helped his second cousin, Charles Cotesworth Pinckney, and John Rutledge, write South Carolina's *Constitution.* Here is one of the articles: *"All persons and religious societies who acknowledge that there is one God, and a future state of rewards and punishments, and that God is publicly to be worshipped, shall be freely tolerated. ... all denominations of Christian[s] ... shall enjoy equal religious and civil privileges."*

Charles Cotesworth Pinckney
(1746 – 1825)

Quotable Quote: *Blasphemy against the Almighty is denying his being or providence, or uttering contumelious reproaches on our Savior Christ. It is punished, at common law by fine and imprisonment, for Christianity is part of the laws of the land."*

George Read
(1733 – 1798)

Quotable Quote: What he and McKean wrote in Delaware's *Constitution*.

"Everyone appointed to public office must say: 'I do profess faith in God the Father, and in Jesus Christ His only Son, and the Holy Ghost one God and blessed forevermore. And I do acknowledge the Holy Scriptures of the Old and New Testament to be given by divine inspiration'."

John Rutledge
(1739 – 1800)

Quotable Quote: Helped Charles Pinckney and Charles Cotesworth Pinckney write the *Constitution* of South Carolina. Here is one of the articles: *"All persons and religious societies who acknowledge that there is one God, and a future state of rewards and punishments, and that God is publicly to be worshipped, shall be freely tolerated. ... all denominations of Christian[s] ... shall enjoy equal religious and civil privileges."*

Roger Sherman
(1721 – 1793)

Quotable Quote: *"I believe there is one only living and true God, existing in three persons, the Father, the Son, and the Holy Ghost ... that the Scriptures of the old and new testaments are a* *revelation from God, and a complete rule to direct us as how we may glorify and enjoy him."*

Richard Dobbs Spaight, Sr. (1758 – 1802)

Quotable Quote: He, Blount and Williamson wrote in North Carolina's *Constitution.*

"No person who should deny the being of God or the truth of the religion [Christian], or the divine authority of either the Old or New Testaments, or who should hold religious principles incompatible with the freedom and safety of the state, shall be capable of holding any office, or place of trust ...within this state."

Hugh Williamson (1735 – 1819)

Quotable Quote: He wrote this when he collaborated on developing North Carolina's *Constitution:*

"No person who should deny the being of God or the truth of the religion [Christian], or the divine authority of either the Old or New Testaments ... shall be capable of holding any office, or place of trust ...within this state."

James Wilson (1742 – 1798)

Quotable Quote: Here's what he and Benjamin Rush wrote in Pennsylvania's *Constitution:*

"We, the people of Pennsylvania, grateful to Almighty God for the blessings of civil and religious liberty, and humbly invoking His guidance, do ordain and establish this Constitution."

Meet the Author

Robert W. Pelton proudly claims a heritage going all the way back to well before the War for American Independence. One of Mr. Pelton's ancestors, John Rogers, came to America on the Mayflower and was one of 41 signers of the Mayflower Compact.

Another, John Smith was one of the founders of Jamestown.

Peleg Pelton served as the fifer in the Continental Army at age 18 during the Battle of Saratoga (1777) and again in Yorktown (1781).

Captain Peter Hager was Commander of the Old Stone Fort in Schoharie, New York, in 1780.

Another, Captain Bezaleel Tyler fought in the only Revolutionary War Battle taking place in Sullivan County, New York. .

Mr. Pelton is a member of the Sons of the Revolution and Sons of the American Revolution.

All of Mr. Pelton's books have been endorsed by the Freedom & Liberty Foundation; Christian America Foundation; and Sons of the Revolution (SOR). For a Power Point Presentation or for book purchases contact Mr. Pelton at 865-776-6644; e-mail: christianamerica2@yahoo.com

Order gift copies of this book:
www.createspace.com/3491125

Other Titles
by This Author

HISTORICAL COOK BOOKS
Cooking & Baking Recipes
From the
War of Northern Aggression
8" x 10" 276 pages $17.95
Order From: createspace.com/3420014

Historical Thanksgiving Cooking
And Baking
5.5 x 8.5   257 pages $14.95
Order From: createspace.com/3578977

Historical Christmas Cooking
In America
5.5 x 8.5   275 pages $14.95

Order From: createspace.com/3486039

A Treasury of Civil War Family Recipes
5.5 x 8.5   235 pages $14.95
Order From: createspace.com/3477320

A Treasury of Family Recipes
From the Time of the War
For American Independence
5.5 x 8.5   255 pages $14.95
Order From: createspace.com/3551835

Baking Recipes and Home Remedies
From The Time of the War
For American Independence
5.5 x 8.5   235 pages $14.95
Order From: createspace.com/3480754

POLITICAL DYNAMITE
Unwanted Dead or Alive
The Betrayal of American POWs
Following
World War II, Korea and Vietnam
5.5" x 8.5" 487 pages $24.95
Order From: createspace.com/3565025

Unwanted Dead or Alive
The Betrayal of American POWs
Following
World War II, Korea and Vietnam
8" x 10" 409 pages $24.95
Order From: createspace.com/3426306

Unwanted Dead or Alive
The Betrayal of American POWs
Following
World War II, Korea and Vietnam
Part 1
8" x 10" 170 pages $12.00
Order From: ceatespace.com/3461216

Unwanted Dead or Alive
The Betrayal of American POWs
Following
World War II, Korea and Vietnam
Part 2
8" x 10" 186 pages $12.00
Order From:createspace.com/3461245

Unwanted Dead or Alive

The Betrayal of American POWs Following
World War II, Korea and Vietnam
Part 3

8" x 10" 132 pages $12.00
Order From: ceatespace.com/3461267

The McCarthy Chronicles
Part 1
Treason

5.5" x 8.5" 445 pages $24.95
Order From: createspace.com/3471179

The McCarthy Chronicles
Part 2
Traitors

5.5" x 8.5" 501 pages $24.95
Order From: createspace.com/3470924

AMERICAN HISTORY BOOKS
Historic Days in 1776
The Declaration of Independence

5.5" x 8.5" 276 pages $14.95
Order From: createspace.com/9426527

**The Prophetic Dream
Of
General George Washington
at Valley Forge**
5.5" x 8.5" 171 pages $14.95
Order From: createspace.com/3427309

**George Washington's
Prophetic Dream at Valley Forge**
5.5" x 8.5" 106 pages $9.95
Order From: createspace.com/3430107

George Washington's Prayers
5.5" x 8.5" 106 pages $9.95
Order From: createspace.com/3569091

George Washington – Chosen By God
5.5" x 8.5" 289 pages $14.95
Order From: createspace.com/3653951

George Washington – Man of Destiny
5.5" x 8.5" 301 pages $14.95
Order From: createspace.com/3491125

Men of Destiny
5.5" x 8.5" 289 pages $14.95
Order From: createspace.com/3693853

HOW TO OR SELF HELP
The Write Stuff
The Perfect Handbook
For Achieving Writing Success
5.5" x 8.5" 445 pages $24.95
Order From: createspace.com/3431896

SURVIVAL MANUALS
Robert W. Pelton's Official
Emergency Survival Guide
8" x 10"   436 pages $24.95
Order From: createspace.com/3485279

How To Survive Anywhere
8" x 10"   437 pages $24.95
Order From: createspace.com/3490509

**Robert W. Pelton's Official
Suburban & Wilderness
Emergency Survival Guide**
8" x 10"   196 pages $9.95
Order From: createspace.com/3476685

**Robert W. Pelton's Official
Suburban & Wilderness
Edible Plant Survival Guide**
8" x 10"   182 pages $9.95
Order From: createspace.com/3478407

**Robert W. Pelton's Official
Suburban & Wilderness
Medicinal Plant Survival Guide**
8" x 10"   177 pages $9.95
Order From: createspace.com/3479026

**Robert W. Pelton's Official
Suburban & Wilderness
Emergency Medical Survival Guide**
8" x 10"   227 pages $9.95
Order From: createspace.com/3480045

Medicinal Plant Handbook
Edible Plant   Handbook
Two Books In One
8" x 10"   436 pages $19.95
Order From: createspace.com/3490255

Orders for Resale
40% Off Retail Price

Send Purchase Order to:

Christianamerica2@yahoo.com